High Moose Alert

POEMS FROM VANCOUVER, THE YUKON AND ALASKA

Rick Lupert

High Moose Alert

Copyright © 2025 by Rick Lupert
All rights reserved

Ain't Got No Press

Design, Layout, Photography ~ Rick Lupert

This book is protected under the copyright laws of the United States of America. Any reproduction or other unauthorized use of the material or artwork herein is prohibited without the express written permission of the author except in the case of brief quotations embodied in critical articles and reviews.

First Edition ~ July, 2025

ISBN-13: 978-1-7330278-5-4

Visit the author online at
RickLupert.com

Vancouver is the loneliest city on Earth. I still like it.

- Douglas Coupland
City of Glass

It's the beauty that thrills me with wonder,
It's the stillness that fills me with peace.

- Robert W. Service
The Spell of the Yukon

We need wilderness whether or not we ever set foot in it. We need a refuge even though we may not ever need to go there.

- Edward Abbey
Desert Solitaire

Tomorrow, I'm leaving for Alaska. I'm going to find an ice cold creek near the Arctic where that strange, beautiful moss grows and spend a week with the grayling. My address will be, Trout Fishing in America, c/o General Delivery, Fairbanks, Alaska.

-Richard Brautigan
Trout Fishing in America

Thank you Addie, Jude, Brendan, Elizabeth, The Thread, Tyrell, Heidi, Ainsley, Angela and the entire Y6C-A crew.

"All of This is Normal" (page 11) and "Dinner in Vancouver" (page 62) first appeared in the Kingfisher Poetry 2 Blog (October 8, 2024).

For Addie, who shimmies like the trees in Denali.

PROLOGUE

Last summer in Italy

it was a million degrees.
The internet tells me
it will be in the mid two-digits
when we're in Alaska.
There's no getting around it –
I'm going to have to wear pants
on this trip.

Last summer in Italy

despite promises made
a cow did not lick me.
This summer in Alaska
I'm planning on interacting
with at least one moose.
Attention Alaskan moose –
be on the lookout for me.
I'm eager to meet you.

All of This is Normal

I want to tell you we dropped our kid
off at camp today, but the truth is
he was driving the car.

Our kid drove himself to camp today.
This has never been written before.
We were in the car.

We experienced it. The double whammy
of our boy who used to be a toddler
with cheeks from here to eternity

operating a motor vehicle on the
freeways of Los Angeles, on his way
to eight weeks away...maybe nine –

I can't bear to look at the calendar.
Speaking of bears, we're going to Alaska
where we hope to see one.

Alaska has made no promises. Someday,
we won't be in the car when he drives
from place to place. Someday he won't even
live in our house. None of this is normal.

Surviving the Ride to the Airport

So far, our driver to the airport
drove through a red light

crossed a double yellow line into the carpool lane
used his phone to show me his website

and was ten minutes late.
Nice guy, though.

Turns out he lives in our neighborhood
which is going to make the review awkward.

He runs over a lot of the bumps that
indicate you are too close to the next lane.

His rearview mirror is a screen that
displays a video of what is behind him.

Finally, we're moving past this outdated
reflection technology.

When he's not driving, he trades foreign currency.
Both careers must be going well.

He interacts with the hand pedal
like a heart attack.

Someone in the next lane uses their turn signals.
Our driver accelerates. No one gets in on his watch.

He has coffee.
I want coffee.

I Was Here Before

I want to show Addie the parking lot
where I waited for her, for hours,
when I got her flight time wrong,
but we've already passed it,
so that opportunity is gone.

Flair Airlines

Don't do it.

On The Plane to Vancouver

I
Row 32 is the last row of the plane.
This is what I have earned thanks to
Flair Airlines and the supervisor at the gate
who only knew the word *can't*.
Addie is in row 11. The air is different up there.
Oh, Canada...may your upcoming
maple delights erase the memory of this.

II
The flight attendant asks for everyone to
speak to them *with kindness*. The unspoken
backstory to this remains unspoken.

III
Now, announcements in French.
Thank God for the French language
making us completely forget Los Angeles.

IV
I will pay double to
never have to utter the words
Flair Airlines again.

V
And now the war for the armrest
with a stranger begins.

VI
They're building a *better LAX*.
I don't know what they're going
to do with this one once it's finished.

VII
Last row.
Will take forever to deplane.
I hope Alaska isn't closed
by the time we get there.

VIII
I'm not sure what Flair Airlines
has a flair for. Operating an airline
is not one of those things.

IX
We'll all get there in the end.
I just wanted to get there
in the beginning.

X
I would like to remind everyone
that Canada is a different country
which makes this an international flight.

XI
There's a convenience to
sitting by the bathroom.
The smell is not part of
that convenience.

XII
Captain Chad
first officer Matthew
flight attendants Katie and Aubrey.
Never a more Canadian Caucasian
flight crew was there.

XIII
One more time in French
they keep saying.

XIV
Hawaiian Airlines
may have the most beautiful
airplanes in the world.

XV
I would like to tell you about the ocean
but, all I have knowledge of are the tops
of the clouds above it.

XVI
One thing of turbulence –
I measure turbulence
in *things*.

XVII
I'm not better than
anyone else on this plane.
Five more syllables.

XVIII
Seated next to
Captain Spread Out Everything –
arms, legs, mouth, cough.

XIX
The last flight we were on had
inter-seat communication available
on the seat back tablets. This flight
doesn't have that, and I know for sure
they don't allow smoke signals.

XX
I hear a clanging bell
like a train is coming
here in the sky.

XXI
There it is again
followed by two things
of turbulence.

XXII
The very last row of the plane.
Is this what my ancestors toiled
four hundred years in Egypt for?

XXIII
I can see the ocean now.
Where was it four-hundred miles ago
when I needed it?

XXIV
Much of what America eats
is grown on the fields
laid out below me.

XXV
I take three pictures
of the single mountain
snow-covered land tit
somewhere between
Los Angeles and
Vancouver.

XXVI
Ten minutes later I see
the other land tit. Different size.
The earth has had some work done.

XXVII
They don't ask my row if we
want any snacks or drinks.
They lost their passion for this work
somewhere around row 15.

XXVIII
It is beautiful outside this plane.
It is also beautiful in seat 11B.

an evening in
VANCOUVER

On the Ground in Canada

I
I met Addie in Canada
after kissing her goodbye
in Los Angeles and after
leaving Flair Airlines
forever.

II
Waiting for the Uber –
It says *three minutes* for many minutes.
Longest three minutes of my life.
But, you're with me.
I'd spend an eternity
in three minutes
with you.

III
Once we arrived in Canada, and partially disrobed
Addie and I discovered we were both wearing
Pink Floyd T-shirts. This is how two people's blood
flows together, without thinking about it, without
any conversation. It's automatic.

IV
We drive by *Craffles* which may serve
Crab Waffles, Crack Waffles, or
Addie suggests, Croissant Waffles.
We may never know.

At Granville Island Public Market

I
At Hobbs Pickles
the blazing sour pickles
are *good for the gut,*
she tells us.
I've come here to be healed by your pickles, I tell her.
Pickle healing is a thing, she assures me.

II
We show up minutes after the cheese booth closes
which ruins all our best laid second course dinner plans.
The microwaved quiche does not help.

III
Addie can *taste the barrel*
during the whiskey flight
which she assures me
is a good thing.

IV
The *Southern Cask Strength may put hair on your chest,*
says the *mustachioed* bartender at *Liberty Distillery*
which concerns Addie greatly.

Aquabus

I
The Aquabus driver uses both hands
to hold the device for me to pay which
leads to a brief moment when
no one is driving the boat!

II
He is a young Canadian boy,
and I only say *young*
because I am old.

III
The giant steel mesh ball
yonder up the creek
has me wondering.

IV
We pass another distillery and
Addie wags her finger no.

On Land in Gastown

A sign in Gastown says
soon we will be walking on water.
I'm not sure if they're planning on
JesusIfying everyone or if they're
preparing for a Noah-like situation.

Late One Night in Vancouver

It is late in the evening in Vancouver,
British Columbia, Canada.

So far, no moose have been spotted
except the carvings in the tourist shops.

The first-world trauma of the airplane seats
has been diffused by the architecture

of this place. Buildings seemingly
haphazardly put together with Jenga-like

impossibilities, adorned with nature
and ready to move in. We have eaten

some of everything, though if an emergency
arises, the Japanese hotdog place with

ample vegetarian options is next door
and open until three in the morning.

Our son, back in Simi Valley, has been
spotted wearing a baseball cap

which can only mean one thing.
We're just not sure what that one thing is.

Did I mention we are on a boat?
They call it an *Aquabus* and it is

big enough for a handful of us.
We consider it a practice boat for

the immense one to come. We're planning
on eating more of all the food tomorrow.

You can count on hearing all about it.

VANCOUVER
day 1

Good Morning, Vancouver

It is morning and the trees on top of the nearby
Vancouver buildings are beaming down at me
inside my Hilton window.

Vancouver is a city of nature, the guy who
drove us here from the airport said. Or
maybe he said *city of outdoors.*

Either way, they have it here, a downtown
with nature coating the architecture.
It initially confused the moose

until they rediscovered the forest.
Down in the lobby, moss adorns the walls.
They spray it once a week. That's a fact

directly from the sweet young man with
a sweet young mustache who checked us in
and wanted to make sure we had *the very best.*

It is two minutes before it is my turn to
coat myself with water and immerse myself
in the other details of the morning routine.

Then the donuts of Vancouver will be my…
well, oyster doesn't sound exactly right.
The donuts of Vancouver will be my donuts.

There we go.

Vêtements

Pickle underwear
and coffee t-shirt.
You heard me right.
Vancouver, I'm ready
for anything.

Walking to the Donut Walking Tour

I
*Is it 'cuckoo' for this way
and 'cheep cheep' for that way*
Addie asks, trying to interpret
the *you may walk* noises.

II
Meat and Bread
is the name of one store.
I'll have the bread.

III
Every Day Foods is the name of another.
Thank God we've arrived on a day.

IV
Of and About Posters
is the name of an art exhibit
happening nearby.
I hear there's an entire room
dedicated to scotch tape.

V
Take home a piece of Canada
one storefront window suggests.
Do I get to pick which piece?
I see a mountain I like.

Underground Donut Tour

I
Coffee is on our tour guide Ainsley,
she gives us the special donut credit card.
When I return it to her, coffee in hand, I tell her
she is now the owner of the store.

II
The lemon poppyseed donut
at *Lucky's Donuts*
is out of control.

III
Vancouver used to have a monorail
but they sold it to England
where you can visit it today.

IV
The nine o'clock gun,
a relic from a time gone by,
doesn't always go off on time,
but it always goes off.

V
Some Vancouver Island residents
take a float plane to work in the city
every day.

VI
They have the highest *off the ground*
air traffic control tower here.

VII
They have a floating *Chevron*
and they used to have a floating *McDonald's*
but that now floats in disrepair.
Location unknown.

VIII
At Giovane Cafe –
one knife is no match for the donut
Ainsley is cutting. It breaks into 3 pieces.
Ainsley has never experienced this
weak of a knife before.

IX
We are doing an excellent job
with the donuts, she tells us.

X
We are inundated with
facts about donuts.

XI
The donut has a hole
so it cooks more evenly
is a guess which earns Addie
a *donut rock star* sticker.

XII
Donuts are famously inexpensive to make
but the most expensive donut
is a hundred dollars.

XIII
Now everyone has a donut sticker.

XIV
Breka Bakery & Cafe
has never closed
since it opened.

XV
You can't go wrong with donuts
everyone agrees.

XVI
I've already had too many donuts
and there are four more to go!

XVII
Addie isn't sure if it's sugar
or beard prickles
on my face.

XVIII
The T-shirts here say
Life begins after coffee.
That is also what
I have been saying
in all of my poems.

XIX
Ainsley tells about the donut lassies
who started the *North American donut economy.*
She considers herself a donut lassie.

XX
The city grew around the train station –
the western-most point of the Canadian Pacific Railroad.
It was an accident that it's here as
where they wanted the city to be was too marshy
and everything was sinking.

XXI
Gassy Jack told the Granville lumber mill workers
if they built him a saloon they could drink free all night.
They built it in one night and got to drink for free.
But then, so the story goes, one of them lumber-milled
off their finger the next day.

They named the neighborhood *Gastown*.

XXII
(Spoiler alert)
It's not a real steam clock!

Some Things I Thought After the Donut Tour but Before the Next Thing We Did

I
Addie conducts the steam clock.

II
Does Tim Horton hear a *Who*?

III
Granville Island is located on False Creek.
But I am too filled with donuts to
tell you anything witty about that.

Vancouver Lookout

I
From atop Vancouver Lookout
we can see at least two other downtowns.
The third downtown is the charm.

II
Addie wonders what the spinning W is for
on top of the small Eiffel Tower.
Viva la France, I say.
Wiva la France, she corrects me.

III
We see Stanley Park where there's an aquarium.
I like fish, but Jesus it's too much.
What does Jesus have to do with fish?
Addie asks. *If you give a man a fish*
you'll teach him to eat a meal right then.
If you teach a man to fish, Jesus will
kiss you on the lips, I tell her. She pivots my body
in another direction and says go that way now.

IV
On top of the Lookout the signs give you
a feel of what's in the general direction of what
you're looking at, but it's not too clear what is what.
We can't find the bank building with a clock for example
and we don't see an orca swimming in the sky
above the buildings despite what
another sign shows us.

V
As is our custom
we have gone up a thing to
see what can be seen.

Stanley Park Horse-Drawn Tour

I
Front row – so fantastic view
of Stanley Park and
two horse asses.

II
The horses do not have USB-C ports
like the Lyft did.

III
Molly introduces us to the special horses
pulling another trolley.

IV
Our horses are Jim and Weston.
Jim and his brother Jack are named
after Jim Beam and Jack Daniel's.
They're party horses when off duty.

V
Eight to nine million people
visit Stanley Park every year.
We are just two of them.

VI
Since there are no locals Molly says
we don't have to worry about
any pesky fact checking.

VII
Vancouver first grew in size –
then it grew in height.

VIII
All the horses are neutered geldings.
You can't have horses getting distracted at work.

IX
Stanley Park is bigger than New York's
Central Park and has a better name.

X
The lighthouse is a popular spot
for proposals. Only one person said no
because *the rock was too small.*
It led to an awkward carriage ride back.

XI
Cricket matches can last for five days.
I don't have time for that.

XII
We drive by the home of the caretaker
of the nine o'clock gun.

These days all he has to do is flip a switch once a day.
He lives rent free and has his own gardeners.

XIII
The Lions Gate Bridge is the bridge that beer built.

XIV
They give their horses the best care possible.

XV
We pass a four hundred year old Douglas fir
which has been creatively redecorated
by a woodpecker.

XVI
There are no bear or moose in this park.
What are we even doing here?

XVII
Another tree had
half its bark blown off
by lightning.

XVIII
We pass by Lord Stanley –
his statue anyway.

Two More Observations in Stanley Park

I
Wildlife feeding is prohibited in the park.
Why did we spend all this money on beaver food?

II
I found *Lost Lagoon*.

Walking Back From Stanley Park

I
Just past the bike rental district
we walk by *Jingle Bao* which
of course, causes me to launch into the song.
Jingle Bao, Jingle Bao, Jingle all the bae!

P.S. Jingle Bao is the Lamborghini of soup dumplings.
P.P.S. No one is fact checking that P.S.

II
I wasn't planning on walking all the way back
to the hotel from Stanley Park but it's what
Lord Stanley would have wanted.

III
We pass by a *Mr. Lube*.
No Mrs. Lube required.

Lyft to Dinner

I
Our driver to dinner at *Published on Main*
is the least talkative. I think he got the sense
that our previous drivers have already
told us everything that needed to be said.

II
Tamaly shop spelled with a *y* instead of an *e*
could use our expertise in this part of town.

At Published on Main

Addie says she saw the asparagus *walk by*.
Sounds like it must be really fresh.

Back at the Steam Clock

People applaud the steam clock's performance at 9 p.m. even though the hands we see say *9:02*.

Walking Back to the Hotel

I
I tried to walk by the storefront sign that said
finally a bra that fits without taking a picture.
I got half a block away, before I just couldn't
and had to turn around.

II
We see wild salmon pie in the market.
How wild are these salmon?
Addie isn't interested in my pantomimes
of what they might look like.

III
The Burger family owns a lot of property
in Vancouver. We keep passing by
The Burger Family Restaurants.
I think they're all cousins.

VANCOUVER
day 2

Conversation This Morning

What?
What?
You had a weird look on your face.
You had a weird look on YOUR face.

Does it really matter who said what?

At the Hilton

I
Addie's squeal of excitement
when she saw I was wearing my new pants
was enough to let any blind person
within the greater downtown area know
it was safe to cross the street.

II
The spinning LG logo and "no signal" text
on the TV by the elevators on floor twenty
of the Hilton, instead of helpful information
and enticing photos of breakfast,
really should be looked at by someone.

III
The salt and pepper monoliths
on our table at breakfast were
put here by *the first people*
but our server cannot confirm that.

On the Way to Capilano Suspension Bridge

I
We drive by *The Lost Lagoon*.
I debate whether to announce to
everyone on the bus that I found it.

II
We're driving over a bridge
to get to a bridge. This is
Inception level madness.

III
We pass by a land-based *Chevron*.
I wonder if it's friends with the
floating *Chevron*.

We Have Arrived at Capilano Bridge Suspension Park

I
I say things to Addie which
aren't worth repeating.

II
Addie wants to make sure I don't
drop my phone off the bridge.
I make no promises.

III
New rule. Addie says
No writing poetry on the bridge.
I point to some nice looking leaves
to hopefully distract her from this.

IV
Certainly the most important rule,
she clarifies, is to not let her fall off the bridge.
This is one I will pay attention to.

V
Addie wonders if I'm lying when I tell her
these trees are called *Stanley Firs.*
I think of it less as lying and more of
stating facts which aren't true.

VI
They say the Capilano Suspension Bridge
can support the weight of two 747s.
I only brought one with me so we should be fine.

VII
Ollie otter promised me trout
but didn't deliver.

VIII
The yellow slugs have the day off too.

IX
The Vancouver Airport owns four hawks
the person at the Live Birds exhibit tells us
who work 365 days a year to scare away
problematic birds as planes take off.

X
Your feet never have to touch earth
at Capilano Suspension Bridge Park
thanks to all they have built here.

XI
You walk across Capilano Suspension Bridge.
But you also have to walk back
unless you want to live with the yellow slugs forever.
They don't tell you that in the brochure.

XII
To the eyes of the man of imagination,
nature is imagination itself.
              -William Blake

XIII
This is a rainforest.
It is always green here.

XIV
Cliffside Restaurant and Bear
Sorry, *bar.*

XV
The boy who brings us our food
has the beard of a French Canadian
lumberjack in training.

XVI
We're on a Canadian bus
to Grouse Mountain.
You pay without touching.
I haven't touched anything
since America.

I wonder

if I should have my pickle underwear washed
or if the one glimpse of it yesterday
was enough to delight Addie on this trip.

How Much?

We pass by Woodchuck Drive.
Finally we can get that question answered.

At Grouse Mountain

I
They say mountain weather
conditions may change rapidly.
No refunds are given for
deteriorating conditions.
This would be a terrible time
for a tsunami to happen
on top of Grouse Mountain.

II
We see Grinder the grizzly bear
napping in the habitat. First it's
just his ear but for a brief moment
he lifts his head and we can see
his big bear nose. The nose he
uses to forage, to sniff honey,
to know the things he needs to know.
The briefest glimpse of a bear nose
is all we got and all we needed.

III
One woman is on *bear habitat watch*
all day. However much it pays
it is more than enough.

IV
I don't think about my balls too much.
I see them every day, of course, doing what they do.
But today in these new zipper-less pants
I needed to work with them a little more
to make sure what needed to happen
could happen here in this bathroom
on this mountain. I salute you my balls
for doing the work you do and making
at least half of everything possible.

V
They give free *Freezies*
for people standing in the long gondola line
which is nice. You can pick any color you want.

VI
The guy we met on the donut tour said he
was hiking up Grouse Mountain today.
We don't see him and can only assume
he must have dressed in honey and
has already been eaten by a bear.

VII
They're packing people on the gondolas for the ride down.
We may sway into strangers for the next five minutes
and their Canadian and cruise ship sweat.
The crowd *oohs* as we say, like an orchestra
or, if you will, an *oohchestra*.

VIII
Sky gondolas
and canal gondolas
are different.

IX
Fifteen minutes until the free shuttle
back to downtown. When we got here
it was forty minutes but I didn't write this
until now so you wouldn't have to read
such a long poem.

Ride Back to Downtown

I
Capilano Road runs along the Capilano River
and seems like a lovely place to live
except for all the noise from Capilano Road.

II
Am I pronouncing it right?
Is it *Capilano*
or *Capilano*?

III
I wonder if the swallows who return
to Capistrano know the swallows
from Capilano. No one has mentioned
swallows here so I may be
chirping up the wrong tree.

IV
Mr. Lube has joined forces
with *Mr. Wash*? I wonder if
they run in the same social circles
as the *Burger* family.

V
Share the road with
a bicyclist and a woman with
a head and no body
driving a car
is what one sign says.

VI
A lot of people are coughing on this bus.
I'm going to need a *beadlet* infusion.
Unless you're Addie, you may not know
what that means.

VII
Ahh the Jervis Mews!

VIII
You don't have to be a cactus to
dine at the cactus club.
Nor does it help.

Walk Back

I
Addie is tired on the mostly uphill
walk back to the hotel but the
cuckoos and chirps of the
intersection crosswalks are
sufficiently distracting her.

II
I bought insoles
at *London Drug*
in *Vancouver, Canada*
for my *American feet.*

Dinner in Vancouver

A leisurely walk down Main Street
after a vegetarian tasting menu
which can only be described as
a Caligula of flavor I determine
there are many great pizzas to try
in this part of town. My stomach
won't allow for any of them now and
we are leaving on a large boat tomorrow
so it may never happen. But if all
Hell breaks loose, and California
sinks into the ocean and the great
American experiment fails, I know
Vancouver is a viable option.

The Nine O'Clock Gun

Just off to the right
of the floating *Chevron*
from how we see it
standing in *Canada Place*
behind the convention center
next to the *Cactus Club Cafe*
just behind where the sea harbor planes
land and take off to land
wherever there is enough water to do so
at a curve on Stanley Island
pointed toward downtown Vancouver
on unceded land
where tall buildings make it
not us useful as it may have been
sits the nine o'clock gun house
where, in twelve long minutes,
a man who lives on that island
will leave his home
flip a switch
which will lead to a bang
telling anyone who cares
and anyone within earshot
who may not care
that it is nine o'clock in the evening.
This is why we are here
in this exact spot – to hear this happen
as it has happened
necessarily or unnecessarily
for dozens of years.
We're such suckers for tradition.
Nine o'clock is coming
and we are here to experience it's arrival.

Scandal Before 9 O'Clock

A young couple on one level
yells at a man on a lower level.
I think they're making fun of his jeans.
I don't hear anything specific until she yells
"Put your penis away" and her companion yells
"No, take it out." We have learned everything there is
to know about this couple, while waiting for 9 o'clock.

Le Magasin

A store in Gastown is called
Le Magasin which means
in French, *the store*, but
it sounds more exotic
because it's in French.

Dear Vancouver

If you shoot off your
nine o'clock gun at 8:59
you're not helping anyone.

Dear Vancouver

All the clocks on the Gastown steam clock
display a slightly different time
which isn't helping anyone.

Goodnight Vancouver

If I was any more stuffed with food
manufactured here in Canada
I'd need a bigger hotel room.

As it is now we have two rooms
and I'm bumping up against the walls.
Our street, Robson, is the home of

Japanese-style hotdogs.
This is why it is inevitable that we will
eventually move to Robson street.

It is our last night in Canada
until we arrive back in Canada.
But not this city, Vancouver

whose nondescript architecture
couldn't be more descript.
I have a real sense of the place now.

Not so much the history, but which ways
are north and south, and which ways are
east and west. My GPS is chirps and cuckoos.

If you needed to get to the water
I could help you. It helps that the water
is in every direction.

But one of the waters is my favorite.
If you get out a map I'll point it out to you.
We're getting on the largest boat tomorrow.

After waffles and coffee, of course.
No one in their right mind sails to Alaska
before waffles and coffee.

ALL ABOARD

Koningsdam

The name of the ship we're boarding later day is *Koningsdam* which will lead to me saying *koningsdamnit*

a lot.

Good Morning Vancouver

I see your clouds today.
I guess they were on vacation
the last few days. Welcome home.
We're leaving you this morning.
Perhaps this is your way to
indicate your sadness.

We'll miss you too.
You're so close, relatively speaking.
I know a couple who recently went to China.
That must have taken so long.
We could be with you again before
half a work day goes by.

Let's plan on that.

Elevator Things

I
Waiting to get on the elevator
with a couple of strangers on floor twenty.
When it arrives, the woman questions
Floor twenty? Which feels like something
you might ask if you were in the elevator
and weren't sure what floor you arrived at.
I don't make an issue of it, I just don't want
this woman driving the elevator when we
eventually get on.

II
Elevators are the cruise ships of hotels.
In this metaphor, hotels are the ocean.

It's all bear going forward.

I
What's behind the restricted access door
at the breakfast restaurant? Bears.
What does *Koningsdam* mean in English?
Bear. (Trust me.) Who brings our luggage
to our rooms on the ship? A bear.
You tip with honey.

II
I ask if Addie is ready for the amount of bear
that's going to come out of my mouth.
She doesn't answer. *You're not ready.*
Then she reminds me she has a bear
in her suitcase. She's ready.

III
Checking in for the cruise
I would have preferred to use
a bear-ding pass.

IV
Addie's looking for bears.
Now she expects them.
All I want is to give Addie bears.

Getting on the Big Boat

I
All of Human Civilization –
apparently, based on the number of
people in this space, we are not the
only ones who had the idea
of going on a cruise today.

II
We see a glimpse of our ship.
Koningsdam – it's a skyscraper
they've laid on its side to float
along the waterways of the world.
We're getting in a floating building.
I can't emphasize enough how large
this structure is. *Unsinkable*.
So they say.

III
I sing a lot of the Love Boat theme song
which I haven't heard since I was a child.
I remember a surprisingly large amount of it.

IV
As we head to passport control
I remind Addie we will be entering by and
leaving Canada again before this trip is over.
Don't throw away your passport I tell her.
She assures me, with a nod, she will not.

We Are on the Big Boat

I couldn't be any more on a boat.
A floating city block with deck after deck
of things to wander in and out of
(except for other people's staterooms)
Restaurants, a buffet, coffee, pizza, shops,
numerous bars, a fitness room, a spa.
I'm on a boat with numerous elevators.
I have yet to count the number of elevators.
Everything is included (except for the things
which are not included, but they're so easily
added on...they'll be happy to tell me the
new total at the end!) We're still parked
in Canada. I can see Grouse Mountain
outside of our room window...that and
the nine o'clock gun building. To call that
stone shack a building when I'm on a floating
city that could fit a thousand of them
may be an insult to buildings. I don't wish
to insult any buildings or objects or people.
I want everyone to know that I am the least
entitled person within ten thousand miles.
That and I want my luggage to come so
I can put on shorts and go to the fitness room.

Big Ship Notku

This ship is so big
I'm sure you can see it
from wherever you are now.

More Shipisms

I
To wash your hands in the buffet area
you put your arms inside two holes
and it happens automatically.
There's a missing instruction about
rolling up your sleeves first.

II
They offer *hands-on facials* in the spa.
The technician wants to know
how many people have a face.

III
When we get off the boat in three days
and many people continue on, will other people
take our room? Should we leave them a note?

IV
I ask Addie if we should take a one-year cruise.
She says no but reconsiders if it could be
hop on hop off and she could periodically
leave for a month.

Addie clarifies she just needs to be on land
and not separated from me. There are many
benefits to leaving for a month.

V
When the tide is out the table is set.

At Billboard on Board

I
The thing is to add "goddamn"to all the songs.
Where's my goddamn salt in Margaritaville
on my goddamned head during
Raindrops Keep Falling on My Head.
It's all songs from the seventies.
Me and goddamned Bobby McGee.
James, the singer, is from goddamned Scotland.
Michelle is from St. Louis, home of the god-
damned arch.
We haven't drank anything in hours.
This is goddamned happening anyway.

II
Dueling piano songs from the seventies
then rock and roll from all sorts of decades
then the blues, shoes and funky. Yeah
I said shoes...I know what I meant.
You could live on a ship making music.
Depending on what kind, the dress code
is fluid. This is floating Beale Street
or floating Nashville's Broadway Avenue.
I haven't found floating Frenchman Street
but enough whiskey and I'm sure I will.

At the Blues Club

The singer doesn't do a great Kurt Cobain
impression but he makes us forget we're at
The Blues Club and gets everyone singing
hello hello hello hello.

A DAY AT SEA

Brunch

I
At brunch in the main dining room
they have alphabetized the waiters.
We have *Bayu* and *Bio*. At least that's
what it says on the card at our table.
When our server comes, his name tag
says *Dwi*. Now I have no idea
what is happening.

II
A man named Ricko takes our berry plates away.
I pronounce it *Ree-ko* but Addie says *Rick-oh*.
Either way we do the secrick handshake
and are now bonded for life.

We spot our embarkation photos.

Of the thousands of people on display,
every single one in color, for some reason
ours are in black and white.

We're from a simpler time, Addie and I.
Or is it Addie and me? I'll let the
proofreaders sort it out.

Note to proofreader:
I'm not changing
the above poem.

Thank You

We see
bear earrings
in the shops.
Or, if you will,
bearings.

Conversation Before the Margaritas and Mojitos Class

Where will you be after the mixology class?
At the bow of the ship screaming
I'm the king of the world.
Should I meet you there?
I probably won't be wearing any clothes.
I won't be meeting you there.

A Couple More Notes Before the Margaritas and Mojitos Class

I
It doesn't help that the motion of the ship
already has me feeling woozy.

II
Side note: ocean motion
should be referred to as
mocean.

At the Margaritas and Mojitos Class

I
They prepare the glasses
ahead of time with limes and lemon
and mint.

II
The empty glasses in front of me –
is eight cocktails too many?

III
Jason is the Mixologist.
He wants us to refer to him
as our *drinking buddy.*

IV
The Blue Blazer Cocktail
is the most dangerous cocktail
in the world.

Made by Jeremiah Thomas with
boiling water, whiskey, lemon
blue flame.

V
The father of modern bartending
made these recipes.

VI
The history goes by quickly.

VII
Les takes over to tell us about the tools.

VIII
The shaker has two parts referred to
as *husband* and *wife* because
together they make happy things.

IX
They don't use their bare hands
to touch anything.

X
Also, use a scoop for ice
and not the glass as you
might chip the glass
and a lady will cut her lips
and sue the cruise line
*for four million dollar*s.

XI
The El Drake Cocktail
named after Sir Frances Drake –
a precursor to the mojito
which cured scurvy.

XII
The proper way to muddle
is 45 degrees.

XIII
They shake the mojito to
that's the way, uh huh, uh huh
I like it, uh huh, uh huh.

XIV
I dance to the disco
like I've already been drinking.
I haven't had a drop.
I'm about to have a drop.

XV
*Alcohol may be man's worst enemy
but the Bible says love your enemy.*

XVI
Ginger Rosemary Mojito –
Fresh lime juice
Fresh from the bottle

XVII
I don't think Sarah
is muddling enough.

XVIII
The best song isn't disco
but I like it –
Papaya by Groovy Chick.

XIX
Drinking ginger liqueur while driving
is good for your eyes.

XX
*If the ocean were a ginger mojito
and I were a duck
I'd swim to the bottom
and drink it up.*

XXI
The Margarita
from 1937 –
Tijuana

XXII
Margarita in Spanish means *Daisy*.
But not the flower.

XXIII
*What happens on the ship stays
on social media.*

XXIV
You can't call it tequila
if it's not made from blue agave.
Well you can call it that but
it won't answer.

XXV
*You can add more liquor.
Their supervisor is not here.*

XXVI
Sec in French means *dry*
*Just like the feelings of my
ex-wife,* he says.

XXVII
The joke about the muddler
being a battery-operated machine
doesn't get more funny as
I drink more.

XXVIII
The third cocktail song is *Twist*.

XXIX
The food and beverage manager
is now observing so no more extra liquor.

XXX
Here's to the three rings of marriage –
engagement ring
marriage ring
and suffering.

XXXI
The fourth cocktail is a version of the margarita
which uses whiskey – Irish whiskey. Sláinte!

XXXII
The Angostura brothers
entered a competition
for the *most bitter.*
Just like his ex wife.

XXXIII
YMCA is the fourth song because Will
who just mixed it, just turned 21.
He's a *young man.*

XXXIV
How do you say cheers in Filipino?
Cheers.

XXXV
Life is a waste of time and
time is a waste of life so
let's get wasted all the time and
have the time of our lives.

XXXVI
And now four lines written after four cocktails
which probably aren't what they said and
make no sense to me many months later:
When your drinking is another days of your life.
When your drinking additional one year of your life.
Drink enjoy and life.
Thanks for all the blessings.

After the Margaritas and Mojitos Class

If you we're interested in a poem
written under the influence of
four cocktails after a mixology class
this is it. I'm not sure the words here
are doing justice to what I'm feeling
but I'm back in my room sliding out of my chair.
I had to pause when writing this to make
a video of me sliding out of my chair in our room.
Addie is somewhere folding butterflies.
We're going to have tea soon and I'm going
to make every effort to maintain the
sophistication required for such an experience.
These line breaks are out of control.
I'm wondering if I should show up drunk
to the origami butterfly class.
The ship is still swaying.
We're all lucky I haven't
thrown my phone into
the ocean.

At Tea While One of Us Is Drunk

I
At least we don't have to save room for the balls.

II
Dwi's mother pronounces his name *handsome*.

IIII
Everyone has balls but us.

IV
We didn't get balls,
I announce at tea.
We'd like some balls.
Please bring us some balls.

V
They are out of coconut balls.
We will not be getting coconut balls.

VI
Something is stuck on the roof
of Addie's mouth but I don't know what!

A Long Poem Written in the Late Afternoon

The seas have calmed as we've moved further north.
Vancouver must have completely given up on
luring us back.

It is late in the afternoon and we've had a full day
of mixology, tea, trivia and walking. We were
successful at all of these things, especially
since we were sharing the responsibilities.

I took care of mixology. We shared tea and trivia.
When I was walking, Addie read a book, but
also walked a little. I'm looking out of our
cabin window and I can see the world
floating by (again it is us who are floating.)

But still no moose, or Russia, or larger
portions of bear. No whales either – and this
seems like where they would be, swimming around
glancing at our ship like it's their mother.

I heard stories recently of packs of teenage orcas
attacking smaller boats, just for fun. I don't know
how you determine the intentions of an orca.
But it has not been proven to me that this is not possible.

There should be visible whales tomorrow.
We are leaving the boat for a day in Juneau, Alaska
in the United States of America, where the whales
will showboat for us while we float around on
a smaller boat. Who knows if I have the
right clothing for this?

Who knows anything except the day of the week
which we only know because it says so on the
floor of the elevators? They change it out every day
just so you know you know.

Ship Walking

I
Every time we walk by one of the pools
I tell anyone who will listen that
the boat is leaking.

II
We see a table on deck 10 with a
large group of the bridge crew eating.
I didn't know they were allowed to eat
and I wonder if I need to get up there
and drive this ship.

Good

The Pacific Ocean is big.
We think we have dominion
over the earth with our buildings
and cities. Even our floating ones.
But the Pacific Ocean dwarfs it all.
The Pacific Ocean will take you.
It will never give you back.

Night

We could have been anywhere on Earth today
contained within this floating Las Vegas.
The views from the exterior decks may
be different, but nothing today was about Alaska.
That's okay, Addie assures me, as the day was
filled with fun and food and food. Most decisions
on a day like today, in this moving place, involve
deciding what to eat, and whether to eat again
after just eating. The music is aces. One singer
pulled Addie up from the audience to dance.
It's not the first time this has happened.
Once you spot an Addie in the crowd, that's
who you naturally gravitate toward. That's
how it worked for me. This could have been
anywhere. I'm sure it would have happened
outside Oconomowoc, Wisconsin. The fact
it happened at sea is all the proof needed.
Tomorrow we will get off this ship.
Then we will get back on it.
Then we will get off it again and that will be it.
At least for the ship. *Moose Watch 2024*
is about to begin.

JUNEAU, JEW KNOW

Good Morning Juneau

Rumor has it Alaska is outside my window.
The ship has calmed down, or perhaps it's
the waters. We've got land on either side of us.

Someone I know is on another deck.
I'm deeply contemplating opening the curtains.
Our feet will touch the American ground today.

A glacier and whales. An old town set up
for people who live nowhere near it.
The world has arrived at my eye steps.

Looking for a Bargain

We paid for a whale watching tour.
But before we get to it, I'm looking out
our cabin window to see if I spot
any extra whales for free.

Vast

Alaska on either side of the boat.
Fog, mountains. I see tails in the water.
It might be whales but their heads
never emerge. For sure, not moose.
The water changes color from dark to light.
The temperature drops to augment the experience.
Behind us, another ship, smoke coming from
one of its stacks. The Russians are chasing us.
Or another cruise ship. Definitely one of the two.
None of this can be seen in Santa Clarita
which has its own beauty, but is interrupted
by buildings and the 5 Freeway. Here,
nothing is interrupted in this vast world.
We are not trapped in the comforts of civilization
if it is not our desire. What else that's available
may not be infinite, but it's more than we
could possibly use.

Inside the Neptune Suite

I
Back in America
a young boy who
likes stomping on living things
may change his pronouns
to *antinouns*.

II
I'm watching the bow of the ship
as displayed via camera on the television
in our cabin, even though it is available
out the window just to the left while
waiting for Addie to get ready so we
can have Dutch pancakes in another
part of the ship. All she has to do
is put on socks and shoes now.
I could stand up and glance out the window
but it is a sitting moment and soon enough
these feet will be on Alaskan ground
also in socks and shoes, as is the
custom of our human people.

III
I've had to pee since Canada.

Koningsdam

I
The carpet in the elevator
tells us it is Monday and we
believe it as we have no other way
to get this information.

II
We take a photo with a talking bear.
The miracles at sea never cease
to amaze.

Bears Moose Bears

I
We pass by a world of shipping containers
somewhere outside of Juneau. I wish
bears were climbing all over them
but I think this is what they use to
ship moose to California.

II
I wonder if bears are curious and
come to see the things the second people
have built. Their noses sniffing the poles
that hold electric cables, wondering
in their bear way, what could these possibly
be for? Their interest wanes quickly
when they see no honey is involved.

In the Tlingit Exhibit

I
You must remember, we treat salmon like
we wish to be treated.
        ~Hoonah Elder James Osborne

II
A boy was adopted by the salmon people.
He stayed there for a few years and eventually
became a salmon. He swam to shore where
his parents saw a beautiful salmon and they
caught him to eat. Eventually they realized it
was their son and they wrapped him in a blanket
and he became human again.

Respect the salmon.

III
I tell Addie next time she eats salmon
to make sure it's not Jude. She says
normally, when they bring salmon
it's already cut and it would be too late.

IV
One elder learned everything he knows
from inside a canoe.

V
Everything has a spirit.

VI
Everyone carves their own salmon hook.

VII
The fish gives up its life for the
benefit of the people.

VIII
The docent has the same jokes for everyone.
It's a small space so we hear them many times.
He is an eagle because his mother was an eagle.
His spirit delights us.

IX
We see people from the boat.
I want to say we should have carpooled
But we did.

X
We see a prizewinning hat.
It is $24,000.
If we want to buy it
it won't be delivered
until September.

Wandering Around Juneau

I
A sign points to *Chicken Ridge*.
That is all the information I need.
Addie wants to know if they
have chicken bathrooms.

II
Our ship is the biggest building in town.

III
We see a cat on the way back from Chicken Ridge.
It's been eating. I can tell. It's eager to be petted
but doesn't want to follow us back into town.

IV
There were no chickens on Chicken Ridge.
Just a neighborhood called *Chicken Ridge*.
I'd like a refund.

V
Addie holds something up in a store
and says it's a *puffy picnic blanket,*
but I heard *puppy piglet blanket,*
which she agrees would also be perfect.

VI
One store in historic downtown Juneau
says *where the locals shop*.
Not local to here, but definitely
from somewhere.

VII
Jellyfish Donuts and Dumplings
is closed for maintenance while
three cruise ships are docked nearby.
This goes against all the laws of nature
that my stomach has dictated to me.

VIII
I just ate french fries
like it was an emergency.
My stomach, filled with
potatoes, tells me *dinner
even later. Dinner will be
a dream deferred.*

Mendenhall Glacier and Whale Watching Tour

I
Our bus is named *Herbert*.

II
The guide tells us the first Europeans here
were Russians. He may not be familiar
with the historic boundaries of Europe.

III
We're already deciding which people
on Herbert we're going to feed to a whale.

IV
Our bus is not decorated like the other buses
but at least it says *Herbert* on it.

V
Dolphin Doug is his name.

VI
Glacier first.
Then boat.

VII
Doug wants us to sell our homes
and collectively buy a shack up here.

VIII
Juneau was ground zero for gold.

IX
Alaskan Doug talks too much.
He was already talking when we got on the bus.
He probably will keep talking long after we leave.

X
We're in eagle country.
Babies wait five years to
get their white heads.

XI
Doug says Lemon Creek's water
looks like lemonade. He may not be
familiar with the traditional look
of lemonade.

XII
The Juneau McDonald's set a record
for burgers sold in a day when it opened
as people flew from all over to bring
burgers back to their towns.

XIII
If we see a bear we are to acknowledge
it has seen more people than we have seen bears.
I'm not sure that is useful information.

XIV
Bears know the sound of human voices.

XV
Addie wants me to acknowledge that Doug
said we should not chase after bears for
a better photo.

XVI
We meet a rock who rode on the glacier for 89 years.
It lives in the visitors center now.

XVII
We meet a plant that survived by paralyzing other plants.

Mendenhall Glacier

Mendenhall Glacier is receding
thirty feet per year since the
seventeen hundreds.

It's cyclical and the earth could turn
this glacier around for any reason.

We don't get to walk on it but
we see it from a close distance.

No bears, despite all the pre-information
about what to do if we saw one.

It is still our first glacier and it was
visible in our eyes. The blue ice –

the pieces of ice floating around
like the lake is a summer beverage

that's been sitting around for a few hours.
This is the Alaska envisioned.

We are further north than I've ever been.
My layers of clothing, three days after
summer began tell the whole story.

Doug

says *ratabugas* instead of *rutabagas*
but he just eats meat and fish so it's
really not an issue for him knowing
what those things are called.

Captured

I see a bald eagle carry a fish away.
Too fast for my camera. But not for
my electronic pen.

On the Orca Odyssey

I
Our job is to look for blowholes.

II
We see hella whales.
Many babies breaching the water
A sea lion or two.
Captain Paul drives.
They give snacks at the end
while we drive back to the dock.
I'm still full of french fries so
I don't want any of it and anyway
this was meant to be about the whales
and not the snacks.

III
Whales don't have lips.
Thank God for expressive udders.

IV
Whales are mammals and have hair.

V
The description of whale milk
may have ruined sour cream and
froyo for everyone on the boat.

VI
The humpbacks
go to Hawaii every year
for free.

VII
Daddy whales make a screen of bubbles
so mom can give birth in private.
But they dip pretty soon after that.

VIII
They have the world's smallest Costco here.
Ninth wonder of the world, she says.

IX
I was hoping for bears holding bald eagles
riding on top of the whales so we could
get it all in at once. (Moose too.)

X
Paul speaks once, right when we dock
to tell us a whale's body temperature
is about the same as ours.

XI
We're so far north –
if we kept going north
pretty soon we'd be
going south.

XII
Doug is still talking.
Doug...you've got to stop.

XIII
For some reason he's
telling us stories about wolves dying.
Why, Doug? Why?

XIV
Take a breath, Doug.

A Word on Child Whales

Like baby animals of any kind
the toddler whales exhibited an
excitement for just being.
Their parents don't fling themselves
out of the water, flip around and
dive back in (classic whale behavior)
but they do. They have the zeal of youth
while their parents do everything they can
to make sure food goes in their mouths.
Mammals work the same wherever you go.
Take it from a much smaller mammal.

Goodnight Koningsdam

It's our last night on this ship before
we head into the Yukon to try our luck.

We're going to miss this floating civilization.
Everyone knows our names, or

at least they pretend to. Sometimes they'll
use the words "remind me" to indicate

they know who we are though the
immediate information escapes them.

On this city at sea, we have danced and drank.
We have eaten and eaten some more.

The late-night hotdogs of Vancouver became
the late-night pizzas of the Koningsdam.

Everything is nice and we got to sleep
until the whales came home.

Going forward it's all waking up and
moving from place to place. My hopes

for the food are not as high. I'm at the
I hope there'll be food level of hope.

There are cruises that go for a year.
There are cruises you can live on.

Right now we'd settle for another week.
Who's going to know our names in

White Horse or Dawson City? Who's
going to recognize us in Denali? (Moose?)

We have to get up so early, so obscenely early,
I might not finish this poem before the alarm goes off.

SKAGWAY to WHITEHORSE

Good Morning, Skagway

It is ridiculous o'clock in the morning
Vacation Standard Time. We are leaving
this *Neptune Suite* for *Birthright Yukon*.
Skagway is outside the windows with
views of many other cruise ships.
The volume of cruise ships takes up
more space than the town itself.
The credit card company is already
not on our side thanks to the thieves
of April. We have defeated them and
it's on to the Neptune Lounge for
espressos and lattes that come after
you barely press a single button.
Who knows what will be required to
make coffee happen in the Yukon.
All I know is if we're not rich with gold
within the next twenty four hours
it may have all been for nothing.

On the Ship Before Getting Off the Ship Forever

I
The elevator floor tells us it's Tuesday.
Now you know as well.

II
Addie needs a shoe break.
And she deserves one. She
deserves all the breaks that
could possibly be afforded to her.

III
In the rolling stone lounge
where people like us are gathering
they have laid out coffee, water and cookies.

I'm not sure who needs a cookie
at 7:50 in the morning
I just know it's not me.

This is the space where, last night,
we were given a whiskey distilled at a place
that was destroyed by a tornado.

I had to "tornado" three times – the first time
I typed volcano and the second time
it autocorrected to tomato.

I want neither of those things now
but am not conceptually against either.
The bourbon had my name on the bottle

so it was an easy choice. I have no idea
what choices I'll have to make the next
six nights, and which will be made for me.

All I know is two nights ago in this room
I was given *the funk* and I couldn't
be more grateful.

Surprise Umbrella

Addie tells me she likes *all my things*.
She means even the annoying ones, like
the surprise umbrella I needed her to find
a space for after she had already carefully
Tetrised everything into the day bag.
*The umbrella was a surprise to us all
my love, and there's no one's things
I'd rather commingle with than yours.*

The Knifeys

The bus to our first stop is delayed
because one couple has to get knives
back from security. That's twenty minutes
less in Skagway thanks to Mr. and Mrs. Knifey.

In Skagway

I
You can wander into Canada
without knowing you have done so.
They're that close and almost no one cares.

II
We see large chard growing
out of the Skagway ground.
[Start Fancy Voice]
This is where we shall dine tonight.
[End Fancy Voice]

In the Skagway Visitor Center Museum

I
Little better than hell on earth.
          ~Superintendent Samuel B. Steele
               Northwest Mounted Police, 1898

II
Chew. Spit. Smoke. Repeat.

III
I had $.35 when I set foot in Alaska.
If I could turn back time, I'd do it for nothing.
          ~ Walter Peterson

IV
The gold was there, lying thick between
the flaky slabs of rock like cheese in a sandwich.
          ~Pierre Berton, Historian

V
No one pretends to follow the changes that are going on here.
Those who have been here a week are old timers. When the next boat
arrives, people will ask questions of us in return.
          ~ Tappan Adney, Journalist, 1900

Wandering Around Skagway

I
Rock Me Momma
plays in the
popcorn emporium.

II
The big question is
should we buy
moosejamas?

III
Not all organ donations are voluntary.

At the Gold Rush Theater

I
Old timey music live on the piano
comes before the show.

II
She plays the slightly out of tune piano
(*part of the charm,* Addie says)
under the watchful eyes of a moose
from a time long gone.

III
Jefferson Randall "Soapy" Smith and Frank Reid
shot each other for no good reason.

IV
Addie and I both get on stage at
The Days of '98 show –
me, because I'm a *good man*
her because they need women
to do the Can-can. Dawson City,
where we're headed tomorrow
is the Paris of the North, they say.

Lunch at the Skagway Brewery

I
That is the color salmon should be,
Addie tells our server.
Yes it is, she says.
She says it twice.
Yes it is.

II
I tell Addie they use live bears
to catch their salmon.

What do the bears get out of it?
They get to keep every other fish

and at the end of the day they get
a jar of honey.

III
After lunch, which included a
vegetarian beer and cheddar soup
we are escorted to the third floor
by the owners who show us their
aeroponic room where they grow
all the produce which sometimes
goes directly from there to salads
within a few minutes, just like
they grow food in outer space.

She Looks Young!

Kayla, our driver, gives detailed instructions. She assures us she is old enough to drive and can usually reach the pedals *most of the time.*

The White Pass Railway

I
was built to make it easy for fortune seekers
to go from Skagway to where the gold was.
By the time most of them made it
the gold was no longer there, but
at least they got to go on a train.

II
*There are more rocks than river
in the Skagway River* Addie remarks
as we stop at Denver Station
so hikers can exit the train.

III
Is a bear driving this train?
I can't tell.

IV
They used almost all their dynamite budget
to blast through Rocky Point.

V
Gold or no gold
this train ride
is gold.

VI
The US Customs border office
is 12 miles from the border
because Americans didn't have
the stamina to make it all the way
up the hill to the border.

VII
Black Cross Rock
is where two men were killed when
crushed by a large black rock.
Too heavy to move, their remains
left there, and a cross put on top
of the black rock.

VIII
Bridal Veil Falls falls
6,000 feet. These mountains
make Santa Clarita feel
like a shack.

IX
I see a train hundreds of feet up
coming down where we will soon
be going up. I hope they remembered
to build two sets of tracks or else we're
going to have a north and south going
Zax situation.

X
Journey (that's her name) is only
accepting US cash...or gold
for the souvenirs.
I'm running low on both.

XI
We're twelve miles from the ships
but can see them from here.
That's how clear the air is
and how big the ships are.

XII
Many horses perished
at Dead Horse Gulch
mainly because their owners
didn't bother...

XIII
We pass by the old bridge –
an engineering marvel of its day,
now broken in the middle, impassable.
Fortunately, we're taking the new bridge.

XIV
We have entered Canada
again.

XV
I don't see any fish in the many streams,
rivers and creeks we are passing, which
may also be why I don't see any bears.

XVI
A young forest is
making its way skyward.

XVII
The water is flowing the other way now.
Once you reach the summit, the water
has to make a choice.

XVIII
The old telegraph poles –
no wires now.
Their time has passed.

XIX
Such beauty on land
created by biological happenstance
I have not known until now.

XX
Addie is missing her chocolate-filled panda cookies.
I wonder if the chocolate is the panda's brains.
When I ask Addie she asks what's wrong with me.
I really want to tell her if you think about it
what else would you expect pandas to be filled with.
But she does not let me continue speaking.

Onward to Whitehorse via Carcross

I
The Fraser bathrooms at the end of the train into Canada
have *American Standard* sinks in them and
the water comes directly from glaciers.

II
Alaska has three million lakes
which is a lot, Carrie says.
This is the kind of insightful commentary
I was hoping for.

III
They want me to keep my jokes to myself
when the border patrol agents board the bus.
Yes, no, and *Whitehorse* are the only things
we should say. I think they're forgetting
how many famous funny people are from Canada.
Do you know Bill Murray Captain Canadian Canuck Face
are not words I should utter.

IV
Time has jumped forward again.
My phone has no service but
it somehow knows when I am.

V
What ship did they kick you off of?
the Border Patrol Agent asks.
Yes, No, Whitehorse, I dutifully answer,
as instructed by my superiors.

VI
The Chilkoot Pass was known as
the golden staircase to heaven.

VII
Lake Laberge is thirty-one miles long
and five hundred feet deep. Its fish
are small because it freezes over and
there isn't much food. The fish do not
eat each other.

VIII
We miss seeing a bear because
the bus ahead of us scared it away.
I hear it was a big brown one.

IX
Addie instructs a wasp to not get on the bus
using hand signals which, I assume,
the wasp understands.

X
If you see a little white spot that looks like snow
and that snow moves, you have just seen a mountain goat.

XI
She tells a long story but the one thing I remember from it is
"we have a lot of big telling around."

XII
Carcross used to be called Caribou Cross.

XIII
They have a rock lady
who sells rocks.

XIV
We drive by the world's smallest desert.
It's surrounded by the worlds largest Canada.

XV
We see a hitchhiker on the way to Whitehorse
and I yell *be careful it's a shaved bear*
which Kayla finds funny enough to say into the mic,
which is essentially the Yukon way to re-tweet things.

XVI
We sing along with *American Pie* on the bus.
I know all the words from when I was younger
and learned all the words. I am not crying.
Nobody is crying. This is pure American joy
in the heart of the Yukon.

At Night Market Ramen in Whitehorse

Addie puts on
an outfit of napkins
to protect herself from
vigorous ramen slurping.

Giorgio's Cucina in Whitehorse

has *all day pasta*. I'm more of a *just in the evening pasta* kind of guy.

Love in the 98 Bar

We walk into the 98 Bar on Wood Street.
The first thing that happens is Billie Janeen

tells Addie she is beautiful. They hug and photos
are taken. We order two shots of local whiskey.

At our table Billie Janeen's aunt, *Darling*, asks us
if any Yukoners still come in here. We ask her if

she is from the Yukon. *Seventy years* she says.
Then, yes I say. Billie Janeen is now complimenting

Addie's ass and posture (in that order).
She refers to Addie as a snack.

I don't know if these people are Yukoners
but you don't get more local than this.

Beavers and bears on the walls.
This place, from 1898 – a hotel on top.

Our patriots are across the street.
Addie draws something in Billie Janeen's memory book.

She is spending a year without a phone.
Now Billie Janeen is drawing Addie.

The bartender pours us exact shots
of *Two Brewers Whiskey,* distilled here in town.

This is where you come
to be in this place.

Goodnight Whitehorse

It is 11:30 at night and the sun has no idea
what it should be doing. Fully available to
our eyes and the *blackout* curtains are
only blacking out our sensibility.

We have to put our luggage in the hall
at another time which goes against
everything we believe in.

In thirty minutes we will have been married
for twenty years. Minus the several hours
until the afternoon when it all went down.

I remember us greeting people as they
arrived at the venue, surprised to see us
but happy to be welcomed. We're not
big on grand entrances, just each other.

Wednesday's grand entrance is coming soon.
Of course, there's a poem on the hotel desk.
Not this one. We're flying from one part
of the Yukon to another.

Maybe we'll strike gold.
I already did.

There May Be Gold in
DAWSON CITY

Good Morning Whitehorse

Six hours have passed since the
calendar read *yesterday*.
The sun has been with us all night.
Tim Horton's sits on the counter

waiting for our mouths. We may not
have coffee until an airplane flies us

to where the gold is. I have beaten
my alarm by six lines of poetry.

I have so much water to put on my body
before this celebration of twenty years

gets off the ground.

On the Bus

Tyrell has donuts for everyone.
We, being the seers of our time,
have already eaten donuts.

We drive by *Mr. Barbershop*.
His wife is a Caribbean restaurant
that was closed last night.

It's a quick forty minute flight
to Dawson. Another group's
bodies will join us on the plane.

I don't know what they are the
Mister and Mrs. of. I just know the sun
has never left our presence.

Airplane Stories

I
They tell us about Dawson's Sour Toe Club
where you take a shot of whiskey with a
mummified human toe in the glass. I love whiskey
but not so much toes. If you swallow the toe
it costs thousands of dollars. There's a book
which tells the history of each toe.
Who wouldn't want a whiskey with a human toe in it?
Tyrell asks. Addie raises her hand.

II
Tyrell tells us the story of
how a flight attendant rescued
his clipboard from international customs.
He said his entire job is his clipboard.
Anyone could do his job
if they had the clipboard.

We've Arrived in Dawson City

The driver tells Tyrell to wait
before making announcements
because the nearby bus has
the same frequency. Tyrell
agrees because he doesn't
want them to know his secrets.

We're a couple hundred kilometers
from the Arctic Circle. This time of year
The sun never sets.

It used to be you could only get into Dawson
by boat. Then the highway came and the age
of the paddle boats came to an abrupt end.
You can go to see the paddle boat graveyard
in the forest if you'd like.

We touch lips over the Klondike River
like two Jack Londons in love.

The Klondike and Yukon rivers met here.
They haven't left each other's presence
ever.

When in Dawson drink the toe.

I overhear someone in the
breakfast room at the hotel say
I had my hole and I lost it.

A History of Jack London as Told by Angela at the Jack London Museum

Jack published 50 books within 17 years.
I have a lot of catching up to do.

Our guide apologizes for going on.
Please go on, I tell her.

Jack worked in a pickle cannery
seven days a week when he was fourteen.

Jack wanted to be an *Oyster Pirate*.
I don't know what that is but feel
it has also always been my dream.

Jack became Prince of the Oyster Pirates.

Then he became a hunter of the
Oyster Pirates for the fish patrol.

Jack steered a ship through a typhoon.

Soon he joined a group of hobos and
became the train riding Frisco Kid.

Angela calls congress *parliament*
and pronounces the *s* in Illinois.

Jack became a socialist at Berkeley
in response to *unrestrained capitalism.*

Jack was twenty-one when he
arrived in the Yukon.

He started prospecting when it was
forty below Fahrenheit – when the moisture
would turn to ice, creating an *ice fog.*

After a while he had to purge himself from the Yukon.

*They are going to publish me
whether they want to or not.*

He was rejected over
one hundred and fifty times.

He was the first writer to make
a million dollars in his lifetime.

Jack was imprisoned in Japan after
fighting a Japanese soldier while as a correspondent.
The American president had him pardoned.

You can't take Jack London, Angela says.

He died at forty.
So I've already made it.

We hear a dog bark outside.
Is that Buck?

His 48,000 square foot mansion in Sonoma
burned down two weeks before he was going to move in.

*I am so tired of writing that I'd cut off my
fingers and toes in order to avoid writing.*

*The function of man is to live
not to exist.*

Angela used to be the Toe Captain.
Her family used to own the toe business.
We get a whole other talk about the many toes.

*Another lie from big toe
Toes R Us.*

Almost Food Before Gold

We fail to eat at what may be the best restaurant in town thanks to them not being open for dinner on Wednesdays and poor timing which led to ice cream ahead of our scheduled time to make our fortunes panning for gold.

Panning for Gold With Brenda

I
The new post office is across the street
from the original post office.
Brenda wishes it was the other way around.

II
Water. Gravity. Agitation.
It's how you get the gold.

III
You have to melt the permafrost then
build a shaft before you get the pay dirt
before you could *water, gravity* and *agitate.*

IV
The stampeders were replaced by dredges
which lasted until 1966.

V
*Now is the modern area of gold mining
thanks to modern equipment
and the rising price of gold.*

VI
A gold claim is $10 (Canadian).
You don't own the land.
It's just a permit.
The government takes
two percent of what you find.

VII
A moose is promised
if we pay attention.
I pay attention but
no moose is delivered.

VIII
I hear they provide
rubber boots.

IX
I expect, even with boots,
my butt will touch a creek today
because of gravity and agitation.

X
I tell Addie to keep her eye out for gold nuggets.

XI
Sluicing is the art of combining
water, gravity and agitation.

XII
After much explanation we are now going to
clean the dirt away from the flecks.
I'm already picking out expensive accoutrements
to fill my mansion with.

XIII
She asks if we're okay with
the presence of dogs. We are
all okay with this.

The dog will bark if it sees a bear.
I've needed a dog bear since the
onset of the first permafrost.

XIV
We did, in fact, find gold.
Both of us. About six flakes each
after standing in a creek

with the dog barking just in case.
The gold, out of the pan,
onto our dry fingers

into a tiny water-filled glass bottle,
sealed with the help of
expert gold digger Lorraine.

The fact that Brenda had
replaced the gold flecks
in the dirt trays for each of us
means nothing.

We have gold now.
Drinks on us tonight.
Just not one with a toe in it.

XV
The bumpy road on the way
in and out of the claims area
reorganized my innards like
heavy gold flakes sifting
to the bottom of lighter silt.

XVI
We're going to build a
small creek in our backyard
so the salmon will come.
It won't be attached to
another body of water
but salmon will find a way.
Maybe bears too.

XVII
We arrive at a paved road
and are ready to convert to
whatever religion that provided it.

Anniversary Dinner at the Aurora Inn

Addie folds a butterfly with the place setting wrapper
while I drink Canadian wine – a Merlot I chose.
It was either that or the Chilean Cab... when in the Yukon.

This was not our first choice but that place isn't open tonight.
We are still each other's first choice which is what counts.
We're dining with lumberjacks or maybe gold miners.

The music may be CanPop. I don't know if that's a thing.
I ordered *The Vegetarian Dinner.* That's what they called it
so there would be no confusion. We are the nicest dressed

people here. Possibly within miles. Sorry, *kilometers.*
The electricity goes out halfway through our meal.
Many people leave the restaurant.

Addie becomes a chicken while imitating
an earlier in the day ketchup squirt.
Should I turn over the table? I ask Addie.

I don't see any reason to do that, she says.
*Should I stand on top of the table in the middle of the room
with a ketchup bottle and squirt it every direction.*

She doesn't want me to do that, but she would enjoy it,
as long as she didn't get ketchup all over her. The electricity
comes back on. We leave the restaurant.

Toe Slogan and Information

I
You can drink it fast.
You can drink it slow.
But your lips must touch the toe.

II
$2500 fine for swallowing the toe.

Diamond Tooth Gerties

We're here now because they have
the Two Brewers *peated* we wanted to try.

We try it. They only take money, but any kind
of money. The show starts in a half hour.

This whiskey won't last that long. *Pace yourself,*
Addie says. It is noticed the old-timey piano

has an electric keyboard inserted where the old-timey
keyboard used to be. They say the shows get more

risqué as the evening progresses. We're at the
very first show so I may have to stand up and show them…

Addie stops me right there. I don't know what else we're
going to do for this half hour. Get ready, Dawson,

for the full Rick Lupert experience. Before I can do anything,
live jazz commences. It's good. It's better than

touching a mummified toe to my lips. Everyone in town
is in this room. We lose track of the jazz as we start to

count the trips we've been on since we've been married.
This is now one of them but it wasn't when I wrote it.

The men's bathroom condom dispenser is out of condoms.
So it's either been a busy night or someone's not doing their job.

Some of the men in our group end up wearing Can-can dresses.
This was always going to happen. There was never a way around this.

Goodnight Dawson City

Dawson City, Canada only has one paved road.
We walked it today but mostly the unpaved ones –
the just-dirt ones – the ones which made me wonder
if I found a shovel, could I dig up the road?

Some of the buildings, or at least one, sunk
because their occupants melted the permafrost
beneath them. I never thought about the word
permafrost until today when much of what I did
was look at it. I'm at a point in my life where
I could tell you what permafrost is.

This is new.

It is midnight and still light outside.
This is the land of the midnight sun.
That sounds like poetry, but I'm just
quoting what I heard.

Tomorrow we go to the second largest city in Alaska.
I'm an international traveler many times over
on this trip alone.

Tyrell tells us it's *just a place*, whereas
the next place is *the destination*.
He said that about the last place relative
to this place.

I'm a huge fan of places.
I can't wait to meet the next one.
And the next.

FAIRBANKS, ALASKA

Out of a Little Hole

Among the first words I hear this morning
and the last in Dawson City, Yukon Territory,
Canada - are *I don't like drinking coffee
out of a little hole. Who does, darling?*
as we unfold our coffee box lids to hopefully
arrive sooner at a desirable temperature
for the very little time left we have
in this magnificent nation.

It's Not a Poem Unless It Mentions the Moon

One person is excited to go back to America *where they have the moon.* This far north may be the land of the twelve noon moon. I don't know that I'll ever see that with my own eyes. Now that I think about it the moon is out in daylight all the time where we live. My eyes are in for a round the clock moon feast wherever I go in this wide world.

Blatant

In case I forget, *Richard* was the name of the man in Carcross who owned the maple syrup shack where we had the delicious maple butter and where we discovered the existence of Two Brewers Distillery which we've now sampled three whiskeys from. (This is more a note for me, but you can't go wrong trying any of these products.)

Compassism

We're going to be one hundred and twenty miles from the Arctic Circle when we arrive in Fairbanks. Uncomfortably close to going south again.

Tyrellisms

Anyone can sleep on Tyrell's bed
when he's not there. He won't share pillows though.
He doesn't want to smell anyone else
when he's sleeping. Also, food is just sustenance.

Goodbye Canada

As this plane's wheels
leave your ground,
your forests and
forest fires, your
kissing rivers,
your gold, your
Jack London.
You only had him
briefly, but he was yours.
Goodbye, Canada –
we're Alaska-bound
where the moose and bears
don't need passports
where the glaciers
have never heard
of passports.
Au revoir, Canada.
Your leftover dollars
in an envelope
for next time.

Seventeen Syllables

There's Tyrell with
his clipboard making sure
everything is possible.

Seventeen More Syllables

I sleep in the plane
while writing this. I sleep on
the plane while writing.

In Flight

I
A flight attendant
laughs like a
baritone chipmunk.

II
We fly by snow covered mountains
and a recently frozen river toward
eighty-three degrees Fahrenheit Fairbanks.
The arctic is peeking at us.

III
Because of the time zones
we land at the same time
as we take off. This is how
you slow down everything
to an actual stop. Eternity
is available to everyone.

IV
We have to sit on the plane
for a while because America
is not ready for us.

I Found This in My Notes and I Know It's Not True

Gastro is very similar to *restaurant*, and I think I just peed on a stranger's bed at the Westmark in Fairbanks.

Fairbanks Ice Museum

I
They say we can touch, sit on
or lick the sculptures. The last one
was my query and it's a *yes*, but
at our own risk.

II
Carver is carving.
Five more minutes.

III
He carves a moose into
a block of ice besides two
fir trees, while singing something
in his native tongue.

IV
It looks cold in the carving room.
I haven't yet committed to
my outer layer.

V
This man works in a freezer
for a living.

VI
Addie *ooohs* when he adds snow
to the ice carved mountain.

VII
They provide winter coats
before entering the main room
Because cold.

Mine is green. Addie's is red.

VIII
We are the Christmas Jews
come to see the fantasy snow land.

IX
It's in an old theater.
Now the balcony seats
display a frozen world.

X
We take pictures on moose.
Behind an ice bar,
We sled. We both sled.
We never get to sled.

XI
We return our coats
and head out to
summer heat Fairbanks.

The Exhibit at the Morris Cultural Center

I
Sometimes we even mow our lawns at 11 PM.

II
Gone fishing.

III
Don't let their scrawny appearance fool you.
These sticks, for us are often one hundred years old.

IV
In Athabascan culture women of childbearing age are strictly forbidden to talk about or look at bears, nor can they touch or eat bear meat. We must avoid bears at all costs.

V
Wood frogs spend the winter in the state of suspended animation.

VI
Honey, please don't forget to plug the freezer back in when it warms up in April – Mom.

VII
You know it's the end of winter when the snow is wet enough to make a snowball.

VIII
Morris Thompson has a toddler in Tanana, Alaska. "When he was a little boy, kids would come by and ask him if he wanted to play outside. He'd say no, I'm going to read books because I'm going to be a big man someday. That quote from my father's past is my favorite."

~ Nicole Jordan

IX
Addie tells me she used to have a few pairs
of moccasins when she was a child. If you are
learning this for the first time, then you are having
the same experience that I had in the
Morris Cultural Center.

X
The tongue on the picture of the sled dog
could put almost any other mammal with a tongue
to shame. In terms of tongue contests.

Except for, perhaps, giraffes.

XI
How much does the average moose weigh?
You never ask a lady moose such a question.

XII
At the end of the exhibit we come across hundreds
of attraction brochures. I tell Addie to look for a solo-
nighttime-after-drinking bear encounter
while I head to the washroom.

XIII
There are two pages labeled *Bear and Moose Safety*
in the 2024 Alaska activity guide, but no pages at all
on where to find them.

We Drive to the Riverboat

I
The driver asks how long have we been in Alaska.
We just came from Canada, does that count?
a woman from our group asks. *No, Alaska and
Canada are not the same place pretty much at all,*
he responds.

II
It's a man's full-time job to make the
blueberry donuts. Our driver holds the record
for eating the most blueberry donuts on the boat –
twelve. It is not our hope to break his record.

III
The riverboat is three stories tall and
there are dozens of donuts on every floor.

IV
All of the narration on the drive to the riverboat
is about our driver's weight and how many
cookies and donuts he has eaten at the
tourist sites in Fairbanks.

V
The roads are paved here.
God bless America.

VI
I see a *Caution Moose* sign.
In my dreams, sign. In my dreams.

We Have Arrived at the Riverboat Compound

I
Should I buy a T-shirt at the gift shop?
By the time you read this, it will be
too late for you to answer.

II
I call *sugar muffin* across the gift store
to get Addie's attention. A man turns around
and looks at me. *Not you, sir,* I say to his
disappointed face.

We Are on the Riverboat

I
This boat is only four stories.
Hardly a Koningsdam but
it's fine.

II
Dog on canoe
Human too.

III
The captain promises to keep us
inbetween the trees where we belong.

IV
The life jackets only have one hole.

V
The river is only 39 inches deep
so the life jacket demonstration
is only so relevant.
Oh, no we're sinking! Pfft. It's over.

VI
Our narrator has trick-or-treated
at twenty-seven below zero.
He's a Fairbanks lifer.

VII
*If the deckhands can't solve your problem
they've been well-trained to empathize with you
with great compassion.*

VIII
Cripple Creek was the most
gold-bearing creek in the entire state.

IX
The big house on the left
is owned by the narrator's ex-wife
and he doesn't want to talk about it.

X
One out of every eighty Alaskans is a pilot.

XI
He's sure we've noticed
the construction style of the houses,
which is there is not one.

XII
The average age here is twenty-eight.

XIII
The Reagans lived in this house
for three whole days.

XIV
Jack McManus' house is to the left.
Was he famous? No he's just a guy with sign.

XV
*Alaska - where men are men
and women win the Iditarod.*
            ~Susan Butcher, Iditarod winner

XVI
The wheel for this much newer boat,
The Discovery III, was built in 1904.

XVII
We almost sail over some ducks
but then they remember they can fly.

XVIII
It takes a minute to teach them to go
but a year to teach them to whoa.
                ~Susan Butcher

XIX
We stop in front of an Iditarod dog kennel
to see puppies and watch some land mushing
with a talk by Susan's daughter from on shore.
Addie and I both weep.

XX
No one uses the word *Eskimo* here
in favor of more specific self-describing terms.

XXI
Caribous shed their antlers every year
The ones we see are reindeer.

XXII
This is the largest glacial-fed river system in the world.

XXIII
We're going the same direction as salmon
when they *get the urge...*
and that guy on deck one.

XXIV
Deanna, the Chena salmon woman
is a native, and her name means
            happy bird.
She's never had fish head soup,
a delicacy just for the elders.
She's not old enough.
We'll ask her again
in 40 years.

XXV
Moose are solitary
and travel alone.

XXVI
Here moosey moose
is the demonstrated
moose call.

XXVII
We see live caribou and dogs and
are told about how it was *a long time ago*
and how it was *an even longer time ago.*

XXVIII
I don't try the sockeye salmon
fresh from the ocean, smoked with brown sugar
they give out, but I would if I was someone else.

XXIX
Native jet skis and
satellite dishes.

XXX
In the winter they can use the ice roads
over the river until the first guy falls through.
Then they don't do that until next winter.

XXXI
Smooth air
Calm water
Clear trail
Godspeed

My checklist of animals to see on this trip

is almost complete if you count the nose of a bear. All that's left is moose, and the many taxidermized ones I've seen so far definitely don't count.

There are 525 fires in Alaska today.

I don't see any of them but the smoke of
at least one of them has filled my lungs all day.

Advice From a Stranger

We hitchhike back to the hotel on another
group's tour bus as our bus, code name *Moose,*
didn't show up. Moose keep avoiding us.
It happens to be this group's last bus ride
and we experience all their farewells and
nice words. It's too soon for this level of
melancholy but it's good practice, I guess.
I've already been weeping because of
the dogs and the caribou and the baby ducks.
What a day. *Pack your ulu, your curved knives,
in your check-ins,* the stranger tour guide
tells us all.

Would You Like to Know Our Plan?

Wine.
Cheese.
Whiskey.

Now you know our plan.

At Library Bar & Bites

I
After two overcooked dishes
we order whiskey and the cheese board
because we're thinking like bears and
winter is coming.

II
I tell Addie she has some *dark* on her face
which leads to her wiping it off with her napkin
and she sees just a little speck of dark
in the napkin and I assure her it was a larger
smudge of darkness. This poem brought to you
by High West Campfire Whiskey.

Goodnight Fairbanks

My lips dry, my hands dry
my stomach and heart full
Fairbanks full

My tongue on ice bear
My eyes on antlers arch
My *Trout Fishing in America*

We rode river
We smelled reindeer
We pet dogs

We riverboat
We happy bird
We blueberry donut

We maple syrup friend
We wine and cheese
We whiskey

My lips dry, my hands dry
Everything else wet
Like Chena River

TO DENALI

Good Morning Fairbanks

The check-in app tells me
there's a lot going on inside the hotel –
other places to mark my presence.
I may have time to, for the record,
put a map pin in the breakfast room,
the gift shop, the scale model
of another ship reminding us of
our recent past. But that's about it.
Fairbanks was barely a quick
peck on the cheek, but it's a single moment
I won't forget.

Imagined Conversation

In my mind I have a lengthy conversation with
our server to explain that if Addie wants tea
she should be able to select from all of the available
tea bags since they were all sitting next to each other
and not just the Lipton black even though she
was confident the other, more interesting tea bags
were reserved for the "grab and go" which
is all fed by the same kitchen that supplies
the food for our table. Look, a twenty three dollar
mediocre breakfast buffet is no one's friend
when the biscuits are biscuit-shaped bread rolls
and the eggs have seen another century and
the berries left their sweetness with the Reagan
administration and the watermelon has
lost its reason to live and the potatoes
have been shunned by the rest of the
root vegetable civilization. I have to be honest,
the coffee was decent. At least there's that.
At least my metabolism has the encouragement
it needs. I'm on a bus. I'm going away.

Out of Control

Ian assures us he is old enough to drive the bus
just as Cayla did. This is the main joke of
Alaskan interior bus drivers.

He adds in he was able to ditch science class
to be here with us. It's a nice tag. We all
participate in the safety speech.

The red door button is not named Henry.
We are sitting on the fire extinguisher and
will be happy to *put anyone out*.

Ian can't promise but we may see bears.
If we don't see three bears he will buy us shots.
One of our group tells everyone to put on blindfolds.

Our group is out of control.
I wouldn't have it any other way
as we go on our way.

Bus Trip to Denali

I
We hear the story again of how
a man named Santa Claus was elected
mayor of North Pole, Alaska.

He wasn't running for mayor.

We heard this story yesterday
when Ian rescued us from the river cruise.

II
While in the bus bathroom
I hear that Ian is talking but
there's no speaker in there
so whatever knowledge he
imparted is lost to me forever.

III
We're driving through a valley
that used to be a hill until
the gold dredge hoses
blasted it all away.

IV
It's not the driver's fault.
It's not the coach's fault.
It's the asphalt.

V
We're on high bear alert.

VI
The locals keep moving the
scenic route signs. It's all
a scenic route.

VII
I didn't call this book
High Bear Alert
but I thought about it.

VIIII
There could be bears behind
any of these old growth trees
waiting for honey handouts
cataloguing human activity.

IX
We drive by *Skinny Dick's Halfway Inn*
but it's company policy to not talk about it
so Ian directs us to look at the trees
on the other side of the bus.

X
The firefighters have a
let it burn policy.

XI
A sign says *no shooting from roadway.*
I say no shooting from anywhere.

XII
They clear the roads between
the asphalt and the trees, so
it's less likely you'll hit a moose.
We're in moose country.

XIII
It's no fun to harvest a moose
at 2:00 am, but if you've added yourself
to the *Roadkill List,* that's when the
call may come, and if you want the moose
that's when you'll have to go get it.

XIV
Moose are the largest members of
the deer family – like our 7-foot cousins
who live in New Jersey.

XV
We enter Nenana, Alaska
Nenana means good place to
stop between two rivers.

XVI
Newspaper headlines in the
Nenana State of Alaska Railroad Museum
say *We're in!* signifying Alaska's
entry to the US as a state. I want to say
welcome to the locals but I fear
I'm too late.

XVII
There's the Nenana Gazebo
where we'll get married tonight!

XVIII
We finish with Nenana in less than
the half hour allotted. They brew
root beer here but it's too early for that.
The train is here. But not enough time
to explore the museum. The golden spike
the president drove into the ground
our only memory.

XIX
Next stop Denali –
but not before we get these
bees off the bus.

XX
They'd be in for a shock
flying out in Denali with
a hundred fifty miles to fly
back to their hive.

XXI
Ian –
driver
bee killer

XXII
Osprey and crow nests
in the electric towers.
You can build infrastructure
but nature doesn't care.

XXIII
I would put out honey sandwiches
for the bears.
(And build a swimming pond.)

XXIV
A Moose will total your car
just to spite you.

XXV
The people of Ferry, Alaska
line up on the side of the train tracks
every year on the Fourth of July
to moon the train as it goes by.
God bless America.

XXVI
I tell Addie the story of how paper was invented
when we encounter the birch trees with their
paper-like bark. Authors would cut slivers of
these trees to write on. Typically, it was one
book per tree, but if you were writing a longer book
it might be two trees.

XXVII
The 5000 feet high mountain to the right
is not a quarter of the size of Mount Denali.

At McKinley Chalet

I wonder if they have a fitness room here
or do they just consider the six million acres
of wilderness to be the fitness room.

I ask Addie if all bears are named Beary.

She tries to think of the name of *that famous bear.*
We get through *Smokey, Winnie the Pooh, Paddington,*
and more before we get to *Yogi* which was who she was thinking of.
So, *no*, she says, and now I'm wondering if any bears are named Beary,
like the two strangers at this bar who are named Barry.

Puppies at the Chalet

They tell you when they're done running.

I hold *Dos*, a female Alaskan Husky –
eight weeks old. She bites my hand gently
and licks my face with the appropriate
amount of tongue.

On the Denali Shuttle

I
People much older than us,
which is almost everyone,
get on the Denali shuttle.
I have a deep desire to live
at least as long, and terrible fear
of being that old.

II
I'm looking deeply into the forest for eyes.

III
We see the aurora borealis
on the bus driver's phone
while he has a couple minutes
to kill at bus stop.

IV
And, emerging from the forest –
up ahead a clearing reveals
a human vehicle parking lot.
So much magic in Denali.

At the Denali Dog Sled Kennels

I
We wanted to mush huskies
but they cancelled us out.
One guy tells of his recent experiences.

II
They're so excited to be picked to pull the cart.
There is much barking and jumping.

III
The dogs are the happiest federal employees you'll ever see.
(2025 addition – and among the only ones still employed.)

IV
They also work in construction –
not with hammers and heavy equipment.
They bring the materials.

V
They love to run.
They have to love to run.

Dogged Out

After sled dogs yesterday, puppies
this afternoon, and more Alaskan Huskies
we may be a little dogged out.

Bring out your moose and grizzlies, Denali.
Bring out your timber wolves.
I see your birds and mountains.

I'm ready for wild encounters.

Lost Time

The timeline in the visitor center shows "11,000 years ago" and then "1898." Feels like they skipped a lot.

This Kind of Sheep They Have Here

When you say *dall sheep* out loud
it sounds like *doll sheep*
if you pronounce it correctly.

High Moose Alert

I ask every
stranger we meet on the trail
if they are a moose.

Todays Program

9:00 am   A butterfly will enter your backpack and be with you through the day.

11:00am   A deep dive into moose scat.

12:00 pm   Forage for lunch. Food not guaranteed.

1:30 pm   Forest nap. Vertical against a birch tree.

3:15 pm   Write postcards to the aurora borealis.

5:00 pm   A bear will eat you.
Meet behind the visitors center.

News From Civilization

Our boy at camp back in California finally gets to be on the red team for *Color Wars*. This has always been his dream.

At Prospector's Pizza

I'd rather have videos of animals
and aurora borealis instead of sports.

P.S. Why don't they call it the aurora bearialis?

Two Stores

I
One gift shop has a banner that says *northern lights,*
as if you could go into the store and buy them.

II
One store sells *crepes and gifts* –
So basically you could buy a bunch of crepe.
(Please say this poem out loud for Maximo effect.)

Music in the Square

Sitting in Denali Square
surrounded by mountains which
put anything else that use that word
to shame...a man and his wife

play old songs because that's what they do.
Joni Mitchell into Johnny Cash.
We're also a man and a wife
who sing songs so this resonates with us,

even this song about the man named Sue with the part
about part of his ear getting chopped off
in a fight with his father. If you haven't
heard this story song before that's a spoiler

and I apologize. We all sing along to
Sweet Caroline. They knew we would.
Everyone always does. *Leroy Brown*
ends the festivities. They'll be back tomorrow

at 5:30 in the afternoon and
every day all season. They don't mind.
They live just up the hill.
It's an easy walk.

Only One Capital Letter

It is bright o'clock in the evening
and one of us trying to sleep
and another one of us is writing poems
and one of us is battling the five lumpy pillows
and one of us is making a fort with the blackout curtains
and one of us is hyperventilating
and one of us hung their pants up on a moose hook
and one of us is not bothered by the noise
and one of us is bothered by the noise
and one of is the noise
and one of us falls asleep
and one of us doesn't

Goodnight Denali

I have to wake up in seven hours and
these mountains are still prying my eyes open.
A midnight woodpecker or a settling building
or a startup compressor are making their
presence known. Denali is everything that
cities are not. Cities are everything Denali is not.
I swing both ways when it comes to cities
and the majesty of nature.

Tomorrow is our *best chance* to see
bear and moose. So far it's been puppies
and adult puppies and chipmunks
from the land-based mammal kingdom.
Whales have been tiding me over for
half a week now. Denali doesn't favor
one species over another – not predators
nor prey. What happens in Denali
stays in Denali, as has happened
even before the first people set up
their tents. Long before western contact.

Goodnight, Denali. I'm too tired
to tell you anything else.

into the Denali
WILDERNESS

High Moose and Bear Alert

Today is the day bear and moose
will do their wilderness dances for us.
Into the tundra, hours on a school bus
where we will be schooled. Heading
toward Denali which used to have
a Caucasian name but only for a
brief time before America came to
this one sense. (Quick update: America
lost its mind again.) We are miles closer
to that massive native peak to, if the clouds
agree, afford us a single glimpse of it.
There are no guarantees we'll see
anything but bus seats and trees.
We're praying so hard though for
natural cold noses. For everything
this holy arctic desert has to offer.

We Are Not Them

Everyone and everyone's mother are waiting to get on buses to the train depot. We're waiting for a bus to take us into the trees.

Tundra Wilderness Tour

I
Rule number one:
Never feed or approach wildlife.

II
The driver has no idea what we'll see today.
What we do see is for our eyes and our camera
lenses only.

III
Brian has been giving tours for nineteen years.

IV
The Nenana River is the boundary of the park.
There are no fish in this part of the river
so if you see anyone fishing, they're not from
around here and they're going to be there
for a while.

V
We're on the only ride in and out of the park.
Mile 43 is our destination.

VI
The animals don't pay attention to the sounds
of the buses. Otherwise us humans should
shut the hell up.

VII
This is the second highest road in Alaska.

VIII
Beautiful time for the wildflowers, Brian says.
Addie nods.

IX
The park exists to protect the dall sheep
among other reasons which have come along
over the years.

X
We're 70 miles from Mt. Denali
when it comes into view,
We have joined the 30% club.

XI
*All humans are drawn to high places
even if they scare the bejeezus out of us.*

XII
We stop to let a family of Alaskan Willow ptarmigan
(the Alaska state bird) cross the road. Mom, dad
and stubborn babies who aren't sure what this
weird river road is.

XIII
Have you ever heard a ptarmigan go to the bathroom?
No? Because the p is silent.

XIV
Brian tells us about the birds we are seeing as we
approach a ranger station. A ranger will get on the bus
at this point, the farthest we could go without a permit.
Addie hears that the birds will come in the bus –
the first disappointment of the day.

XV
Animals are more important than humans, here.

XVI
We get off the bus to see Denali
formerly known as McKinley
formerly known as Denali.

A 39 mile glacier sits between two peaks.
I could *crush it with my fingers*
but it's bigger than everything.

Everything I've seen.

XVII
We're approaching the Sanctuary River.
The last river was the Savage River.

XVIII
The Eskimo potato is not actually a potato.
The grizzly bears don't care.

XIX
Never run from a bear.
It's a test to see if you are something to eat.
You do not want to pass this test.

If a moose charges you, you run.
If you see both a bear and a moose
Brian has no idea what you should do.

XX
We stop at a city of restrooms
next to the Teklanika River.

XXI
When we cross the Teklanika Bridge
things are going to change for us.

XXII
We hear from another driver
there's some bear scat on the road.

XXIII
The only cat out here is the lynx.

XXIV
We pass the bear scat
exactly in the middle of the road.

XXV
More bear scat.
The bears are punking us.

XXVI
A woman yells *moose!*
But it's just a bush.

XXVII
We see a cheese pizza
which is what they call
the ground squirrels
the bears eat that have
about as many calories
as a medium cheese pizza.

XXVIII
We see Denali again –
This time only fifty miles away
above the chromatic mountains.

XXIX
A grizzly bear is seen, but
not with my eyes. So small.
So far away.

XXX
I don't want to be
the boy who cried
moose.

XXXI
Final stop.
An hour back to the chalet.
I'm hoping for a Moosetember surprise.
This would be funnier if it was one
of the months that ended in *ember*
and not June.

XXXII
Brian's giving us a free book.
I'd rather have a free Moose.

XXXIII
The drivers have a series of
hand signs to indicate to each other
what animals they've passed.
This would be an excellent
job for Addie.

XXXIV
Back on paved road
My dreams of moose
smoothed over.

XXXV
We get a consolation caribou
towards the end.

XXXVI
There are more moose in the
metropolitan Anchorage area
than in Denali. Now they tell us.

XXXVII
We're getting back into civilization
and cell phones will start working.
Brian tells us *soon we'll hear the
ringing and the binging and the dinging.*

XXXVIII
Addie wants blueberries now.
She's going full bear.

Addie kisses my lips at the shuttle stop.

Ooh cold lips...did you just drink water?
No.
Let me try it again.
For science?
For science.

Concerns

I
The warning sign says *High Moose Activity.*
Promises, Denali, promises.

II
What do beavers do after they finish their dams?
Retire?

III
High Moose Activity
turned out to be
no moose activity.

Funiculopolis

They should build a funicular
from the lower part of the
McKinley Chalet to the upper.
Addie says I would put funiculars everywhere.
Correct. I would carpet the world
with funiculars.

Athabaskan Lessons

I
Na means river in Athabaskan.

That's why all the rivers end in na
Chena, Nenana etc...
If a river doesn't end in na
it was named by a white person.

II
Hello, goodbye, and *holy crap* in Athabascan
is *Chenab*...but ChatGPT and Google Translate
don't agree with that so who knows what I heard
back in June of 2024.

The Bizarro Tyrell in the Princess Lodge

We walk into the neighboring resort where we
snuck on the shuttle to get closer to ours and
I expect to see a slightly off Tyrell helping people
who look slightly like us.

We end up seeing a guy with a beard who
could almost pass, and I asked him if he'd be
willing to shave his head for a poem.

Denali Square

Steve and Jen
play the old-timey music.
Steve narrates.

He reminds us
often
that we're in Alaska.

Johnny Cash
starts us off.
They hiked this morning.

The mountain
was out today.
They play the

endless tuning song.
Steve went to Woodstock –
1999.

He looks like
Lars from Metallica
or my ex-roommate, Tony.

Both are a compliment.
*The midnight sun will
make you do weird stuff,*

Steve says. Amy doesn't
talk much, but when she sings
angels enter the canyon.

They're Johnny Cash heavy
and that's okay. In fact
it's really good.

Jen sings *Blue Bayou*.
Steve handles the whistling
and the guitar.

Let's keep the
old timey going.
Feel free to

put some gold
in the pouch.
They won't complain.

The Music of Denali

Dinner and a show –
we arrive as early as possible to achieve
the view our height requires.

The dinner is not spectacular
but the biscuits are on point.
Mashed potatoes. Succotash.

The show is spectacular.
Young actors who double as
our serving staff.

They know how to sing.
Some have comedy chops.
They bring us into the story

of Denali and the first people
to walk up one of its peaks.
They pull people from the audience

to gallivant on stage and
pretend to be trees. We speak
to Israelis sitting next to us

about what we all do and eat.
We speak to another couple
traveling for the first time.

All I want them to do is travel more.
Places are the best. Almost any place
that is not your normal place will do.

The show ends. We tip. We leave.
The cast, our performers, our servers
greet us at the door.

We see them later at the bar.
I wonder what their employee
discount is. I wonder

which of them are dating.
We buy the bartender a shot.
He has a mustache which looks

like it could be easily removed and
reapplied. He almost doesn't take the shot
because Maribel is nearby.

Another woman is near us
and talks to us about everything.
Some people are leaving here

and going in one direction.
Others are leaving here and
going in another.

We are leaving here – this resort,
this National park, this Denali.
It is not leaving us, though.

Goodnight Denali

At midnight thirty the Alaskan dusk
seeps into our room through the
blackout cracks. It hasn't learned
to put itself away at night.

to
ANCHORAGE

Good Morning Denali

It is morning in Denali.
The sun has kept watch all night.
Our luggage is already on its way.
If the system continues to work
we will see it tonight. This is
our last day in *the system*
before we are cut loose to
wander the streets of Anchorage
on our own – all choices, ours.
The only thing included is
the midnight sun.
I'm praying a moose will
escort me to breakfast.

Today's Information

Following Tyrell's specific instructions
every time anything is spoken out loud

in the lodge lobby, I assume it has
something to do with me and panic.

I get on the bus first while Addie
finishes her muffin inside.

Tyrell says we'll wait for her
unless I slip him a twenty.

I'm trying to calculate the actual
terrible cost of that.

We have the only driver in Alaska
with a chicken-proof yard.

Why? It's *impeccable*.
I'll take the check now.

Sorry, I'll take the chick.
They're going to take a photo

at the train. Addie is concerned
she's not wearing a photo-ready outfit.

There's no one more photogenic
than Addie no matter what

fabrics she's wrapped around
herself. This is everything I know.

Train Ride to Anchorage

I
The *Rail Gazette* magazine has an article called "parts of a train." The first item listed: windows.

II
They have three restroom rules:
1) Lock the door.
2) Lock the door.
3) Wash your hands.

III
The bartender has
a master's in mixology
and a BS in BS
(Bartending School).

IV
The more you drink on the train
the more moose you'll see.

V
We're ten minutes into
our eight-hour train ride.
It's still very exciting.

VI
There are no moose on this train.

VII
I go to take a picture of the river
on the left side of the train and
miss a pond on the right.

VIII
The north and southbound trains
use the same track. I assume
they thought of this ahead of time
and have some sort of plan.

IX
Many of the trees in this forest are dead.
No one says why.

X
If you see a rock out of place
a glacier put it there.

XI
The happiest woman we've ever seen
walks towards the back of the rail car.
Her smile is turned up to eleven.

XII
We see Denali from the train.
Now it's just showing off.

XIII
As we pass a sign that says
highest point on the Alaskan Railroad
the guide tells us *this is the highest
point on the Alaskan railroad.*
So it's confirmed.
It's all downhill from here,
he adds.

XIV
Forest fire smell on the train
as is the natural way
in Alaska.

XV
I'm not sure if all the coughing
in our rail car is the natural sound
of older people, or if they're
actually sick.

XVI
An older woman almost takes Addie's
seat while she is away instead of the seat
behind us next to her husband.
You don't want to downgrade, I tell her.

XVII
We ride through Honolulu, Alaska.

XVIII
Trip wisdom
Tyrell never lets the truth get in the way of a good story.
Another woman says she's never done anything she's never done.

XIX
Someone throws a paper airplane off the train
from atop the Hurricane Gulch Bridge.
We're as high up as the Statue of Liberty.
Denali is still with us. I hope that airplane doesn't
hit a bear in the eye.

XX
Hurricane Creek flows into the Chena River.
I'm not sure it's called Hurricane Creek but
it's definitely a creek.

XXI
At this moment the success rate for reaching
the top of Denali is 51%. This number changes
all the time.

XXII
WE SEE A MOOSE
and its baby running away
from the right side of the train.

XXIII
We're forty-six miles from Denali.
It's still the biggest thing in view.

XXIV
The mountain is flaunting, today.

XXV
We're passing a big beaver lodge.
But no big beavers. Beavers are
very social and sometimes invite
stranger beavers to live with them
so we're told.

XXVI
Addie says she's tired and then it's like
her switch got flipped off as she collapses
closed eyes against the seat rest, so quick,
no time even for a *timber!*

XXVII
Three hours into the train and still
excited thanks to the moose sighting
of two hours ago.

XXVIII
Addie says she wants a pillow and
before long is on my shoulder.
I wonder if I'm lumpy and if
she plans on fluffing me.

XXIX
The train stops by this tree
for some reason.

XXX
Some time goes by.
We are still stopped by this tree.
It's called *siding* where we go to a side track
so trains coming the other way can proceed.
They did have a plan!

XXXI
They have bear-viewing tours from Whittier
south of Anchorage. I was hoping for free bears.
Always with the add-ons, Alaska.

XXXII
As we sit by these trees for over
forty-five minutes, the train excitement wanes.
I hope they distract me with lunch soon.

XXXIII
Waiting for the train to move again with
no internet or view of anything turns this
into the make-your-own stimulus portion of the trip.
I run through all the lyrics I know to *You Be Illin'*
which is a good chunk of the first verse, numerous times.

XXXIV
While in the dining car another train goes by and
stops next to us. I thought the point of us being stopped
was so the other train could just go by.

I start narrating this experience with
my best Jacques Cousteau accent.
We examine the sugar substitute packets.
Everybody is *illin'*.

XXXV
The dining car is a unicorn robot civilization.

XXXVI
They're out of buns so we get bread
and they forgot the cheese.
I'm not eating until Russia.

XXXVII
Tyrell and I have a conversation
in the train bathroom hallway about
how we're the least important train
in the Klondike. I'm not sure we're in
the Klondike but they serve Klondike bars
in the dining car so we might as well be.

XXXVIII
We're six and a half hours into this train ride.
The excitement is minimal. We're following
the highway to Anchorage and I couldn't
have more bars. Three more hours and
we'll be in Anchorage. I have no idea what
we're going to do when we get there but
I'm definitely going to tell you all about it.

XXXIX
Those million-dollar homes along Nancy Lake
come with their own train horn…no extra charge.

XL
Tyrell tells us we've entered *moose country*.

My passport is ready.

XLI
The Knick Glacier
feeds the Knick River
which feeds into the Knick Arm.
They like to say they're all *knicked*.
In my culture, this isn't as funny
as they want it to be.

XLII
Jen in our group has a moose alarm
that goes off and she starts emitting
moose moose moose moose
from her extra moosery perception
giving you a jolting alert to open your camera
and point yourself in the right direction.

XLIII
Avoid the Knick Arm mud flats.
They're like quicksand and tides could come in.

XLIV
Some of this forest closer to Anchorage
has an almost Ireland-like green.

XLV
The train horn alerts cars at
upcoming intersections to avoid
potential collisions. It also alerts
nearby moose to hide from our cameras.

an evening in
ANCHORAGE

A Moment of Silence

The flags are three-tenths of the way down at the Westmark in downtown Anchorage. Apparently, someone is just not feeling well. A speedy and complete recovery to whoever it may be.

Impression

Anchorage is not a beautiful city but it is surrounded by beauty. Mountains and clouds and waterways where whales are available if needed.

The insides of the buildings could use some updating, but the people inside the buildings, and many of them wandering the streets, have the hearts of Alaskans.

There is a mustiness here. The whole thing could use some updating. But they're too busy catering to us and enjoying themselves in the summer and just trying to survive in the winter.

The Anchorage Pillow Situation

We negotiate pillows
at the Captain Cook Hotel
which hasn't been updated
since the time of Captain Cook.
Too collapsible – A more firm pillow
(which they want me to change to firmer
but I'm sticking to my guts on this one)
is found in the closet. After some
hesitance and silent sleepy agreement
pillows are passed back and forth.
The pillow situation has been resolved.

we already leave
ANCHORAGE
on a moose, bear
and glacier quest

Good Morning Anchorage

I am up earlier than my alarm which
is unheard of in my world, but today is
glacier, bear and moose day

and I'm anxious not to miss any of
those things. My friend Ross is wandering
around Israel in blue pajamas, because

the Middle East has lost his luggage.
They have many other problems over there
so he's taking it in stride.

He would not approve of how the lines
break in this poem and, someday, if
he makes it this far in this book

he will acknowledge this to me.
Sometimes poems written in Alaska
are secret messages, little hidden

treasures to discover. I better wrap
this up as my alarm is going off in
eight minutes, and I don't want to

keep any moose waiting.

Addie Saves Everybody, Again

In a gift shop before breakfast
we see genuine Alaska axes.
I ask Addie if I can bring an axe
on the plane and then imagine
myself running up the aisle
wielding it, shouting *I'm the pilot now!*
No axe for you, Addie says.

Right of Way

Last night four tween hooligans
on bicycles don't yield the right of way.
I guess you have the right of way.
That's right, and he keeps talking
for blocks about his God-given
Alaskan right to run through red lights
on his Huffy. We duck into the Hilton
for sanctuary as is our God-given right
and they head off to the Cook Inlet
still talking about his right of way –
yelling even. It's the next morning and
I'm sipping coffee, and for all I know
he's still talking.

One-Hour Trolley Tour

I
Ace tells us he is our God.
Sometimes when people are mad at him
they call him an *Ace hole.*
He's a true Alaskan, born and raised here.
He's part Athabaskan.
He's the first ginger Alaskan Native.

II
Everything is a five-dollar charge.

III
The largest earthquake in Earth's history happened here –
9.2 on the Richter scale. It split Fourth Street in half for miles.

IV
The original railroad car's job
was to bump moose off the tracks.
The moose, *goosed.*

This was a hundred years ago.

V
The city got its name because
the post office refused to call it
anything else.

VI
The day the Sleeping Lady Mountain wakes up
all war on earth will end.

VII
We see Captain Cook's back.
We'll see his front later.

VIII
On a previous tour, someone answered
moose as Anchorage's number one money maker.
(It's coal.)

IX
It is July 1st.
Fireworks in broad daylight –
coming in three days.

X
No one has to worry about natives
in western Anchorage anymore.
It was a different story a hundred years ago.

XI
We pass by Crabapple Tree Prison.
(Moose love crabapples.)

XII
Mr. Buzzwinkle the alcoholic moose.

XIII
We drive by a three-story underground home.
You have to mow your roof.
The driveway is heated which
they call cheating here.

XIV
The earthquake sunk over seventy homes in
what became known as Earthquake Park.

We take pictures across the tectonic ice plate.

XV
We drive by a moose sanctuary.
It's protected by a moose gate and moose fence.
We don't see any moose.

XVI
Moose eat black spruce.
They can leap over thirteen feet in the air.
We're putting crabapples and black spruce
in our Santa Clarita backyard
to entice the moose to come.

XVII
Ace cannot control the moose.

XVIII
Small planes range from $60,000
to 1.5 million.
I'd rather buy a moose.

XIX
You get one to two years for shooting your husband,
and three years for shooting a moose out of season.
Alaskan priorities.

XX
Ace lets us off the trolley to take photos
even though he's not supposed to.
What happens on the trolley stays on the trolley,
he tells us. *Unless you get off the trolley,*
I offer helpfully.

XXI
Some tours are fast
Some tours are too slow
This one was really well Aced.

XXII
Nasguk – *big head.*

Fire

We hear Denali is shut down because
of a fire, visible from the hill behind
where we stayed. No electricity.
No train in and out. People using
restrooms on bus shuttles in parking lots.

How lucky we were to see what we saw
when we saw it. May Denali be blessed
by the work of firefighters. May its
hidden moose and bear know what to do
so they can make their presence known
for future eyes.

May it always be known as
Denali.

Bus to the Wildlife Center

I
The Denali fire affects us anyway
as thirty new people who were supposed
to go there are now on our bus.

II
We take the hardest right turn in the city.

III
A thousand resident moose.

IV
Moose would lick up the salted roads.

V
All of Anchorage revolves around
its unseen moose.

VI
It's not dirt.
It's dirty snow.

VII
Rachel's uncle got a free roadkill moose.

VIII
They teach how to harvest a moose
in high school. I wonder if they teach
Moose as a second language.

IX
Spenard's is an old-timey Home Depot.

X
Home Depot is like a new-fangled Spenard's.

XI
We should all chip in and buy Alaska.

XII
We're reminded how beautiful Alaska is
when we leave Anchorage.

XIII
Another bus surrounded by coughing people –
Forgive me if I use the next several pages
for my last will and testament. Does anyone know
how to notarize a poetry book.

XIV
One man caught in the mud in Turnagain Arm
was rescued by helicopter. But his swimsuit was
caught in the mud so he was carried on the end of
a rope across the sound with his baby belugas
fully dangling in view of all Alaska.

XV
The Chumash forest is roughly
the size of New Hampshire.
No offense.

At the Alaska Wildlife Conservation Center

WE JUST TOOK A WALK WITH A BEAR!

On the Bus to Portage Glacier

I
Rachel notes, as we pass by the caribou,
the difference between reindeer and
caribou is reindeer can fly, obviously.

II
All the bears are the same species
they just live in different neighborhoods.

III
Next up, Portage Glacier.
The boat gets close enough
so you can lick it (I'd imagine).

At Portage Glacier

I
Rain and low visibility where we
board the boat. Praying for a
midnight sun storm.

II
The boat is called The Ptarmigan.
It's the state's national boat.

III
This forest was established to protect the salmon.

IV
We're on a new lake, formed in the 20th century.
It still has that new lake smell.

V
These mountains were created when
the North American and Pacific plates
collided with each other.

VI
The glacier is receding or
going to meet its nearby friend
The Shakespeare Glacier.

VII
We see many baby glaciers
floating in Portage Lake.

VIII
This blue ice
thousands of years old
carved this valley
made this lake possible.
It doesn't *calve* while
we watch it. That's okay
Let it take its time.
I'm barely the blink of an eye
on a glacier's calendar.

On the Bus Back to Anchorage

I
We pass by a family of waterfalls.
One of them is Siamese.

II
We learn some people on our bus
secretly saw wildlife and didn't tell anyone.
That's okay...I WALKED WITH A BEAR!

III
I adjust the screen so it doesn't rattle.
Addie closes a cabinet that opened up.
The Luperts are fixing everything on this bus.

IV
As we drive further from the glacier
the temperature toward Anchorage
goes up. It may also be the heater
on the bus fooling me, and there will
be a terrible shock when I get off the bus.
but I am grateful for this on-bus summer weather.
Next summer we're going to wherever the equator is.

I Did It With My Face

At *F Street Station*
when it comes to paying
the tap machine is not portable
but our server says she's quick
and I can *do it with my face.*
I opt to do it with my face.
Obviously.

I'm Still Doing It With My Face

I write the *I Did It With My Face* song
after Addie eats fish and chips and a full glass
of house red wine.

Sitting at Bruins on 3rd Street

Advertisements on the TV.
I like it better when the TVs
show videos of bears
and the aurora borealis.

Goodnight Anchorage

People are wandering around the Hilton
at 12:30 in the morning like it's 12:30
in the afternoon. The constant daylight
messes with everyone's sensibility
on when to do things and when not to.
I can't imagine what the constant nighttime
is like when winter comes along. People
doing nothing for days on end while the snow
comes down and doesn't stop. This is a life
so many have chosen up here...so few of them
vegetarians judging by the items on the available menus.
Oh there are options but this is another area where
this city needs to be updated.

We've moved to a different hotel for boring reasons
but this was the plan all along so don't get any ideas.
It's almost as dated as the last one, but the fitness room
stays open forever like the forever summer sun.

Employees are populating the elevators like joyrides.
I don't know if they're prepping for the next day or
don't realize the last one has ended.

The train whistle is perpetual. Two hoots
(is that the right word, hoot? No wait, it's *whistle*
isn't it?) indicating it is approaching an intersection
completely audible on the twenty-first floor where
we have a full view of where the Knik and Turnagain
Arm's kiss. Maybe they didn't meet, but rather have
always been the two arms of downtown Anchorage.

Tomorrow is easy. No specific wakeup. No bags out.
Nothing we *have to* get to. Breakfast, a museum
maybe in and out of the shops. It is our last day.
We have a bonus night at the end of it, and then
we're out of here. Get ready for some heavy
nostalgia about things I'm not done experiencing.
Get ready for nonsense on a plane. It's all coming
on the pages that await you.

Can Sleep

It is 1:30 in the morning.
Outside the window it is nightish.
That's all...nightish.

last day
ANCHORAGE

Biscuits or Donuts?

No alarm this morning.
Just the shuffling of my
forever sweet mate and

the sound of opening
curtains to tell me it's time.
Yesterday's whiskey

reminds me last night
happened. Outside the window
all of Alaska – all of everything.

There are few decisions
left to make in this adventure
where already others

told us what to do more than other
times we've flown from California.
Addie asks, *biscuits or donuts?*

at the perfect time. There is
work to be done. I'm going to
cut this off and start doing it.

In the Hotel Room

I was looking for a different
full-length mirror because I didn't
like what I saw in the first one.

Walk to Moose À La Mode

It snows cotton
on Fourth Street
as we walk to breakfast
at *Moose À La Mode*
which doesn't sound kosher
for at least two reasons.

At Moose À La Mode

The server tells us
she has three sizes of coffee
and gives us the math.
I ask her if she can give me
a visual and she displays
the three cup sizes for me.
When asked what else she does,
she magically transforms them
into a single cup. The coffee
is acceptable.

The Kobuk was established in 1915.

We are here for tea and fireweed donuts.
I brought my own coffee from the Moose place
because we couldn't confirm, with all the resources
we have available to us, if it was any good here.

Inside the door we're greeted by a woman
bearing a sample of tea. She looks like she
is also from 1915 and has one of the best smiles
we've seen on this trip. She tells us about
The Russian teapot which has a word like
semaphore. I wonder if they used to
land planes here. Places change over time
to meet the needs of their communities.

They bring Addie her tea and tell her
just let it steep they have no idea
who they are talking to as Addie already
has her timer out.

It used to be called Kobuk coffee and
now I feel guilty having walked in with
Moose coffee. They did drop coffee
from the store name but, even with
all the resources available to me,
I have no idea when that happened.

Book Titles

I
It's going to take
all my earthly powers
to not call this book
I Did It With My Face.

II
I see a book called *How to Hide a Moose.*
This whole trip may work out after all.

III
I see a second book called *Where Do I Sleep*
which is the question that comes up when
Addie finds out I'm hiding a moose.

At the Anchorage Museum

I
I tell the woman selling tickets
that I am seven years old
and she almost smiles.

II
A wall opens up and
it turns out to be a
giant elevator.

III
Two *Wintermoot* Quotes:

Almost all tongues are
hyrdroskeletal in nature.

Raven put on his stank old moccasins.

IV
An interactive part of the museum
where you can draw, features
magnum sized sharpies...

V
Part art museum
Part science museum
Part history museum
They have picked
all the lanes.

VI
At one point
Addie is encased
in a giant bubble.

VII
Chomper, the live snapping turtle,
seems like he wants to be in a
bigger space.

VIII
The starfish on display
also seem to have
given up hope.

IX
You can't touch the feather bears
on level two but everybody wants to
so bad.

X
Bear so big they
had to use two canvases.

XI
Staring at a giant white wall –
it's a polar bear orgy.

XII
Two polar bears were killed
upon arriving in Iceland.

XIII
Across the street
Renee's Soul Food and
Tito's Gyros are married
in one building.

XIV
I see a painting of
an actual polar bear
in an actual snowstorm
which is much more visible
than a lifetime of blank canvases
has prepared me for.

XV
The first *people* have taken up
western art and they are
very good at it.

XVI
When I die
encase my head
in a drum.

XVII
We see a TV star from South Dakota.
I've always wanted to be South Dakota famous.

XVIII
Norman Bright
is dwarfed
beneath a
huge ice-wall.

XIX
Salmon Spirit Mask
John Hoover, 1980

Very few people go as
salmon spirits on Halloween.

XX
Salmon are gifts.
Every single one a blessing.

XXI
Book cover idea: hanging salmon
with vertical blood lines on
dark blue background
with grungy snow

XXII
We can shoot this arrow up in the air.
I wonder how far it will go?

XXIII
We were a courageous and ingenious people
who had made a rich life under sometimes
inhospitable conditions. ~ Paul Ongtooguk

XXIV
Bear with human butt
outside the museum cafe window.
Muse indeed.

There's also a moose
with a human butt.

This is human butt garden.

XXV
The elevator doesn't work.
We may not survive the stairs.

XXVI
Ways to use bucket: countless.

XXVII
I see a book called
The Hidden Lives of Trees.
Unless it was written by a tree
I'm going to let them keep their secrets.

XXVIII
The docent says there's a thing she
recommends we go in.
We go in the thing.

The thing has beanbag chairs
This is where we live now.

XXIX
You don't hate Mondays.
You hate capitalism.

XXX
Try this:
Sit in the seat.
Hoist yourself up with the rope.
When you reach the top, let go.

XXXI
There is a sign near the
statues outside the museum
of the moose and bear and duck
and wolf with human butts
that says *for viewing only.*
I can't imagine what other purposes
people have used them for.

Gift Shops

I
You're not allowed to have a gift shop in Anchorage
unless you put a life-sized stuffed bear outside of it.

II
Most of the shops offer a free ulu knife with
a minimum $99 purchase. Pretty sure that's
the quickest way for me to chop off all
my fingers the next time it's my turn to cook.

III
The *Salmon Express* trolley goes by.
This is how they travel to spawn now.

IV
We buy Alaska at Buzzwinkle's Bazaar.
Fourteen dollars. We own it now.

I did it with my face

again.

At Fletcher's in the Captain Cook Hotel

After eating a mediocre baked Alaska
and drinking a fine Alaskan distilled bourbon
a woman at the next table reached over to

our table and took one of our menus and
brought it over to her table, without asking,
without any word of acknowledgment.

I almost turned into Larry David and
confronted her about how those were
our menus and she could have at least

asked if she could have one. Addie prevented
me from taking any action but thought it might
be fun to take one of their napkins

without saying anything.
We both agreed we should take
our second menu and put it on

their table and tell them
Just so you don't have to share
but we don't actually do it because

we're not Larry David and we don't want
that to be our last memory of eating or
drinking anything in Alaska.

Walk Back

We walk by a bar called *The Broken Blender.*
Honestly, I'm not going in there until they fix it.

Back

Because of first-world problems
and a night manager who never smiles
we will likely never be returning to
the Hilton in downtown Anchorage.

Goodnight Anchorage

Anchorage, we did the best we could with you.
You gave us bears and moose which the rest
of Alaska could not. Though we did have to
excursion from your borders to see them.
You gave us beautiful views of your Sleeping Lady
and the water between her and us. You gave us
a decent vegetarian Wellington and a new song
and a museum that was every kind of museum in one.
You didn't quite close the deal, Anchorage.
You should run yourself through the committee.
Pay attention to the comment cards, maybe
slap a coat of paint here and there. There should be
moose stationed at every park, that should be
fundamental number one in your constitution.
It wouldn't hurt to turn the coffee up a notch too.
We'll put a pin in the map for you, Anchorage.
Keep us on your email list...we're not against you.
We're just going home tomorrow and you never
popped the question. We might have said yes
but you didn't seem interested. Not once.
I'll give you this...the one place on F Street
where you can walk in and slice yourself some
cheese...even though the sign says not to...
the staff winks and you can just do it. I loved that.
Every establishment could learn from free cheese at the door.
We're heading home tomorrow, where it's ninety degrees.
Maybe this is mutual. We're probably better off as friends.
I wish you no ill will, Anchorage...I'm going to listen to
that song I remember from the nineties that
mentioned your name and try to think of you like that –
always part of my repertoire. Ready when you are.

Blackout Curtains

Not black enough,
Addie says.

HOME
to where the sun sets

Good Morning Anchorage, for the Last Time

I dream we have to take planes and buses and boats
to wherever we're going next. Anchorage's train whistles
wake me into the reality of when and where we are.
It has never stopped being daylight. We need to
get out of this hotel before the night shift comes back.
Good morning, Anchorage. We'll take our breakfast now.
I'm laying everything down on the possibility of your coffee.
Your elevators, so far, have done the work of
Captain Cook. He died in Hawaii long before we had
the chance to walk its probably wild chicken-laden shores.
It's not fair to mention that place at the end of this one.
But it's the only other American place that isn't a lower 48.
So you can see how they're related. It's like they're sisters.
Our entire trip to Alaska was a sibling brunch.
More about the relationship than the food.
Aloha Anchorage. We'll always have Paris.

At Breakfast

I
Addie orders the continental breakfast
at the buffet. I order the hot. She sneaks
one of my potatoes and I decline to report her
to the server out of an abundance of love.

II
Now she wants to take the entire honey bottle home.
I can understand as it's bear shaped. Normally
they give you packets. This is a whole bottle.
It's ours now, she says.

Thirteen Syllables

Haphazard ride to
the airport. Still looking
for moose.

Flying Home

I
We take off and are afforded
one last view of the Sleeping Lady.
Maybe the noise of the plane
will wake her and by the time we land
all the world's conflicts will be finished.
Grateful for airplanes and the
loud sounds they make.

II
Addie is reading her book three seats
and an aisle away. I've learned so much
about the oil inside truck wheels from
the talkative man in the seat next to me.
I should be able to fix anything by
the time we land.

III
Now it's just clouds and the
peaks of Alaska mountains
outside the window.

Last remnants of the vast beauty
we left behind.

IV
I am seated between
the largest man in the world
and the most talkative man
in the world. He taps me on
the shoulder to point out glaciers.
The other one has cheese delivered.
I'm going to focus on the
abundant leg room.

V
They're serving premixed cocktails
in cans. Western civilization
is coming to an end.

VI
The talkative man is not on the same team
as liberal America. Voices his concerns about
immigrants, electric cars, the homeless.
We were both paper boys as kids and
he drives a Saab which was my first car.
A starting place for common ground.

VII
I have to hide my phone from him
because he keeps asking questions
about what's on the screen.

He's had four beers so far.
I've had no beers. Once he caught
an eighty-four pound salmon.

It's mounted on a wall.
He shows me a picture of the fish,
and the family of moose that live

on his Alaskan property, and many,
many pictures of his Saab. His wife
doesn't travel with him or else

her garden would die and who would
take care of mom. He poked me in the
shoulder numerous times to point out

things outside the window, including
football fields. At least a half hour is spent
trying to convince me to get an Alaska Airlines

credit card, and the same amount of time
on where to stay on any of the Hawaiian islands.
When the plane lands he says

have a nice life, I'll probably never see you again.
We deplane in Seattle and I see him head off to the
restroom to see about those four beers he had on board.

VIII
I'd like to switch seats so he and the big man
can make their plans. I'd like to switch seats
so I can sit next to my wife. I'd like to switch seats
so this madness can end.

IX
The first class lady leans her seat back into our row.
Don't they have enough already?

X
It's a two mountain day
south of Seattle. Maybe three
but I'm on this side of the plane.

XI
The third mountain shows up.
It was on this side of the plane
the whole time.

XII
Wow.
Look how much
world there is.

XIII
It is nighttime in Los Angeles.
What could this possibly be all about?

EPILOGUE

Messages to Tyrell Over the Next Year

Tyrell was the tour director on the land portion of our trip. He took very good care of us, but made a point of telling us not to message him once he dropped us off in Anchorage. These are the messages I sent to him over the following year.

Tyrell! We were at the wildlife center
and a moose looked at me funny.
Do I get a free cruise?

Tyrell! We're back home in Los Angeles
but I forgot my ZIP code. Can Holland America Lines
provide me with a new one?

Tyrell, I think you're with another group now,
but would you mind confirming that we were
your favorite group in all history? Please?

Tyrell, it's really hot in Los Angeles.
Can you have the folks at the McKinley Chalet
send us some Alaskan snow?

Tyrell, we're going out for pizza tonight.
I don't need anything from you, but just
wanted you to know where we were.

Tyrell, we're in the Istanbul airport.
Is it okay if we refer to it as *Constantinople*?

Tyrell, I long to put my bags outside of
my room and find them at my next destination.

Tyrell, my Alexa isn't listening to me.
Can you add cheese to my grocery list?
Tyrell, are you sure you don't want me to
have your personal phone number?
Some of these feel important.

Tyrell, I gained two and a half pounds
on the trip. Do I owe Holland America
money for the extra weight?

Tyrell, after three days, I finally showered
for the first time since Alaska. Can you make
a note in my record?

Tyrell, I'm wearing the sneakers I wore in Alaska.
Do I still have to pay California state sales tax?

Tyrell, if you visit us in Los Angeles
do you bring Alaska with you?
We'd like to see it again.

Tyrell, I used the wrong attachment on my hair trimmer
and accidentally shaved off one of my eyebrows.
Can I get a voucher for another one?

Tyrell, they got my order wrong at In-N-Out.
Is there anything Holland America can do?

Tyrell, Addie's out of town for a couple of days.
Do you know where we keep the food?

Tyrell. We're going to Germany in a couple of weeks
for a music festival. As best as I can tell Germany
is next to Holland. Are there any discounts available?

Tyrell, my hair is falling out.
Are you using all of your beard?

Tyrell, where are my pants?!

Tyrell, I need a blood sample and
the last four digits of your credit card number.
There's no time to explain.

Tyrell, I think my left hand is slightly
bigger than my right.
Help!

Tyrell, can you tell
me how many syllables
are in a haiku?

Rick Lupert will return ...
unless the people of Japan decide to keep him.

ABOUT THE AUTHOR

The author and his beloved in front of the Gastown Steam Clock in Vancouver

Four-time Pushcart Prize and Best of the Net nominee Rick Lupert has been involved with poetry in Los Angeles since 1990. He was awarded the Beyond Baroque Distinguished Service Award in 2014 for service to the Los Angeles poetry community. He served for two years as a co-director of the nonprofit literary organization Valley Contemporary Poets. His poetry has appeared in numerous magazines and literary journals, including *The Los Angeles Times, Rattle, Chiron Review, Red Fez, Zuzu's Petals, Stirring, The Bicycle Review, Caffeine Magazine, Blue Satellite* and others. He edited the anthologies *A Poet's Siddur: Shabbat Evening - Liturgy Through the Eyes of Poets, Ekphrastia Gone Wild - Poems Inspired by Art, A Poet's Haggadah: Passover Through the Eyes of Poets,* and *The Night Goes on All Night - Noir Inspired Poetry*. He is the author of twenty-eight other books: *It's Spritz O'Clock Somewhere, The Low Country Shvitz, I Am Not Writing a Book of Poems in Hawaii, The Tokyo-Van Nuys Express, Hunka Hunka Howdee!, 17 Holy Syllables, God Wrestler: A Poem for Every Torah Portion* (Ain't Got No Press), *Beautiful Mistakes, Donut Famine, Romancing the Blarney Stone, Professor Clown on Parade, Making Love to the 50 Ft. Woman, The Gettysburg Undress* (Rothco Press), *Nothing in New England Is New, Death of a Mauve Bat, Sinzibuckwud!, We Put Things in Our Mouths, Paris: It's the Cheese, I Am My Own Orange County, Mowing Fargo, I'm a Jew, Are You?, Feeding Holy Cats, Stolen Mummies, I'd Like to Bake Your Goods, A Man With No Teeth Serves Us Breakfast* (Ain't Got No Press), *Lizard King of the Laundromat, Brendan Constantine Is My Kind of Town* (Inevitable Press) and *Up Liberty's Skirt* (Cassowary Press), and the spoken word album *Rick Lupert Live and Dead* (Ain't Got No Press). He hosted the long running Cobalt Café reading series in Canoga Park for almost twenty-one years, relaunched in 2020 as a virtual series, and has read his poetry all over the world.

Rick created *Poetry Super Highway*, an online resource and publication for poets (PoetrySuperHighway.com), *Haikuniverse*, a daily online small poem publication (Haikuniverse.com), and writes and occasionally draws the daily web comic *Cat and Banana* with Brendan Constantine (facebook.com/catandbanana). He also writes a weekly Jewish poetry column for the Los Angeles *Jewish Journal*.

Rick works as a music teacher at synagogues in Southern California and as a graphic and web designer for anyone who would like to help pay his mortgage.

RICK'S OTHER BOOKS AND RECORDINGS

It's Spritz O'clock Somewhere
Ain't Got No Press ~ May, 2024
The Low Country Shvitz
Ain't Got No Press ~ May, 2023
I Am Not Writing a Book of Poems in Hawaii
Ain't Got No Press ~ August, 2022
The Tokyo-Van Nuys Express
Ain't Got No Press ~ August, 2020
Hunka Hunka Howdee!
Ain't Got No Press ~ May, 2019
Beautiful Mistakes
Rothco Press ~ May, 2018
17 Holy Syllables
Ain't Got No Press ~ January, 2018
A Poet's Siddur: Friday Evening (edited by)
Ain't Got No Press ~ November, 2017
God Wrestler: A Poem for Every Torah Portion
Ain't Got No Press ~ August, 2017
Donut Famine
Rothco Press ~ December, 2016
Romancing the Blarney Stone
Rothco Press ~ December, 2016
Professor Clown on Parade
Rothco Press ~ December, 2016
Rick Lupert Live and Dead (Album)
Ain't Got No Press ~ March, 2016
Making Love to the 50 Ft. Woman
Rothco Press ~ May, 2015
The Gettysburg Undress
Rothco Press ~ May, 2014
Ekphrastia Gone Wild (edited by)
Ain't Got No Press ~ July, 2013
Nothing in New England Is New
Ain't Got No Press ~ March, 2013
Death of a Mauve Bat
Ain't Got No Press ~ January, 2012
The Night Goes On All Night Noir Inspired Poetry
(edited by)
Ain't Got No Press ~ November, 2011
Sinzibuckwud!
Ain't Got No Press ~ January, 2011
We Put Things in Our Mouths
Ain't Got No Press ~ January, 2010
A Poet's Haggadah (edited by)
Ain't Got No Press ~ April, 2008
A Man With No Teeth Serves Us Breakfast
Ain't Got No Press ~ May, 2007
I'd Like to Bake Your Goods
Ain't Got No Press ~ January, 2006
Stolen Mummies
Ain't Got No Press ~ February, 2003
Brendan Constantine Is My Kind of Town
Inevitable Press ~ September, 2001
Up Liberty's Skirt
Cassowary Press ~ March, 2001
Feeding Holy Cats
Cassowary Press ~ May, 2000
I'm a Jew, Are You?
Cassowary Press ~ May, 2000
Mowing Fargo
Sacred Beverage Press ~ December, 1998
Lizard King of the Laundromat
The Inevitable Press ~ February, 1998
I Am My Own Orange County
Ain't Got No Press ~ May, 1997
Paris: It's the Cheese
Ain't Got No Press ~ May, 1996

For more information:
www.PoetrySuperHighway.com

www.ingramcontent.com/pod-product-compliance
Lightning Source LLC
Chambersburg PA
CBHW052132070526
44585CB00017B/1798